The One

Also from
Ben Young and Dr. Samuel Adams

THE TEN COMMANDMENTS OF DATING

The One

A REALISTIC GUIDE
TO CHOOSING YOUR SOUL MATE

BEN YOUNG & DR. SAMUEL ADAMS

THOMAS NELSON PUBLISHERS®
Nashville

Published in Nashville, Tennessee, by Thomas Nelson, Inc.

Library of Congress Cataloging-in-Publication Data

Young, Ben.
   The one : a realistic guide to choosing your soul mate / Ben Young & Samuel Adams.
   p. cm.
   ISBN 978-0-7852-9657-7
   1. Mate selection. 2. Mate selection—Religious aspects—Christianity.
3. Single people—Psychology. I. Adams, Sam. II. Title.
   HQ801.Y678 2001
   646.7'7—dc21   2001030639
                                                                              CIP

Printed in the United States of America

03 04 05 06 PHX 9 8 7

Nicole and Claire
Lacy, Benjamin, and Emma . . .

with confidence that each of you will not just settle for a
partner or a playmate but, with God's leading,
you will choose a true soul mate.

Contents

CONTENTS

Acknowledgments

$\mathcal{W}$e would like to thank our wives, Elliott Young and Julie Adams, for their support, unconditional love, inspiration, and grace along the way. You are our true soul mates.

To Dad, Mom, Ed Jr., and Cliff for a lifetime of love and support. And to my mother-in-law, Jane Hackley, for her constant encouragement.

To Paula and Alex Adams (aka Mom and Dad) for your example, sound wisdom, and advice over the years.

We also want to thank Mike Hyatt, Brian Hampton, Blythe McIntosh, and Kyle Olund at Thomas Nelson for their hard work and willingness to believe in this project.

Special thanks to Toni Richmond, my radio cohost and assistant for going above and beyond the call of duty and for your invaluable insight.

Thanks to Dave Riggle and Glen Lucke, the shallow psychologist and personal theologian, respectively, for their ever accurate insight and relevant input.

Where would I be without The Single Connection radio team of Adrienne Flowers, Bob Boyd, Chris Townsell, and Amy

Cooper reaching out to singles across the country? Thanks for all the years of support and hard work!

To all the wonderful people in Single Life, Single Source, and Single Plus at Second Baptist Church, Houston, for living out a positive and dynamic vision for singles in the body of Christ.

We could not have written this book without the nightly support of Starbucks coffee and the regular supply of liquid inspiration and energy to write this book.

This book is written in memory of my dear friends Kirk Askew and Charlie Davis.

The One

Introduction

~

The
Make-or-Break
Decision

*R*emember when finding love was easy? If someone caught your attention, all you had to do was reach into your school desk, pull out a Big Chief tablet and a red crayon, and write a simple note: *Do you love me? Circle yes or no.* That's it! No games. No bull. It was short, sweet, clean, and neat. When you got a little older, it became a bit more complicated because you actually had to work through a mediator—the person's best friend. There was an art to communicating your intentions for a relationship through another: "Could you please ask Sally if she likes me?"

Nonetheless, the relationship game was still fairly cut and dried. But somehow as an adult, life and love get much more complex. The process of finding love becomes more difficult. The stakes are high, the risks are certain, and the game is serious. In addition, there is a dimension to love and attraction that is difficult to explain. Often, there are deeper needs, unconscious drives, and seemingly random events that can influence our choice of dating partners. Admittedly, there is a mystery to relationships that will never be completely unraveled.

In this respect, we appreciate the struggles that many experience in their search for "The One." We know that the quest for love can be confusing, frustrating, and even intimidating. It is no wonder that the approaches of so many singles tend toward various extremes. For example, some are inclined to be unprepared and thus reactive in their approach, leaving far too much to chance. They seem content to wait for almighty Cupid to strike them with his golden arrow. Another similar extreme is the tendency to overspiritualize the process, leaving *everything* up to God or some other cosmic force. These people avoid their own responsibility in the process, expecting God Himself to lean down from the heavens and whisper the name of The One in their ears.

As relationship counselors, we have worked with thousands of singles and couples regarding their quest for The One. Almost every day we see you in our office or we interact with you weekly by radio. In fairness, many have exercised good judgment and responsibility in their attempts to find a partner for a lifetime. On the other hand, we have seen far too many singles demonstrate a passive or superstitious approach to finding a mate, only to end up empty-handed. We have also interviewed some of the top relationship experts around the country, and they have confirmed the devastation that comes with a lack of proactivity and personal responsibility in the matter of mate selection.

LET'S MAKE LOVE USER-FRIENDLY

This book explores attraction and romance in a realistic way. We will help you appreciate the more tangible and practical side of love so you may navigate through the rough waters of intimacy. Our intent is to clear up certain distortions about love and give you a practical plan to aid in this most important process. We will give you direction to help you develop your ideal picture for a mate, and we'll give you realistic guidelines to help you find a true soul-mate relationship. Quite simply, we want to empower you to take personal responsibility for your dating life and to plan for success in it.

In their much anticipated book *Fear of Intimacy*, Dr. Robert Firestone and Joyce Catlett summarize more than forty years of clinical observations, representing one of the most comprehensive studies ever conducted on intimate relationships. Among their findings, they conclude:

> The success or failure of an intimate relationship is strongly influenced by one's choice of a mate. Selecting a person with the right characteristics is perhaps the most important prerequisite for attaining the ideal of a close, personal relationship.

In other words, your ability to choose the right kind of mate can either make you or break you. Therefore, one of the most important things you can do is to know, in very specific terms, what qualities you should be looking for in a mate; how to attract and identify someone with these qualities; and how to take this relationship to the ultimate place of marriage. This pretty much sums up the focus of our book—helping you to be wise and intentional about your search for a soul mate.

WHAT IS A SOUL-MATE RELATIONSHIP?

We recognize that the term *soul mate* has been used and misused again and again to the point where it may mean different things to different people. Most assume that a soul mate is the one "true love" who represents the missing half of your soul; the special one who automatically and infinitely knows, loves, accepts, and adores you. It's a nice fantasy, wouldn't you agree? The roots of our belief in a soul mate go deeper than the fairy tales we learned as children, promising princes, glass slippers, and magical kisses that could transform life into a happily-ever-after existence. In fact, the origins of this term are found in several places, including Greek mythology, Celtic wisdom, and even Hindu tradition. Nonetheless, please understand there is no biblical or historical truth of its existence, nor is there any evidence of such a phenomenon in the world of relationships around us. Consider the staggering divorce rate. Or think about all the couples you know. How many would you say bear the mythical resemblance of having that one "special" soul-mate relationship?

What are we really saying? Well, we believe the conventional notion of the one true soul mate is really just an illusion that we hold on to in order to deal with life's current difficulties and longings. It represents a false hope that actually works against people in their efforts to create a healthy, lasting, committed relationship. In truth, a soul-mate relationship is one whereby you share yourself with another based upon a connection at the deepest level of your being. In his book *Soul Mates*, Thomas Moore writes, "A soul mate is someone to whom we feel profoundly connected, as though the communicating and communing that take place between us were not the product of intentional efforts, but rather a divine grace . . . We may find a soul partner in many different forms of relationship—in friendship, marriage, work, play, and family. It is a rare form of intimacy, but is not limited to one person or to one form." In the spirit of this definition, we would agree that many relationships can have a soul-mate quality. As such, when it comes to choosing a marriage partner, you should look for someone with whom you can develop a soul-mate relationship, but you should know that there isn't just one person in the whole world who is a candidate. Your challenge, then, is to be proactive and responsible as you choose the best partner out of the many possible life partners.

> **When it comes to choosing a marriage partner, you should look for someone with whom you can develop a soul-mate relationship, but you should know that there isn't just one person in the whole world who is a candidate.**

WHO BENEFITS FROM THIS BOOK?

If you are a teenager, we applaud you for taking the time to consider insights about finding your mate. You are in a stage of life where you have plenty of time to prepare yourself for The One. Just as you are preparing and training for college or a future profession, you should also be in the process of learning to recognize the marks of a healthy relationship and how to make wise choices in this matter. In our society, adolescence and identity formation are still in process until the middle twenties. In his book *Finding the Love of Your Life*, Neil Clark Warren writes, "Statistically, marriages seem to be much more stable when they begin no earlier than the mid-20's." To illustrate, he indicates that the divorce rate for those married at twenty-one and twenty-two is twice as high as that for those who marry at twenty-four or twenty-five. Obviously, the older you are, the more likely you will be to make a wise marital choice.

If you are past your college days and not currently in a dating relationship, this is a great opportunity for you to gain insight and wisdom about what you should be looking for in a mate. You have the objectivity and the luxury to focus on the important aspects of relationship preparation. We will help you understand how to identify a wise choice for a mate and how to be more proactive in your search. This book is just as applicable for you if you are well beyond those college days.

Finally, you may be in a relationship and wondering whether or not it is right for you. Perhaps you are in the early stages and you need help determining whether or not to continue with it. Or you may be in the later stages of a relationship and you need guidelines to help you make that ultimate, lifetime commitment to your partner.

Regardless of your situation, this book can give you clear answers to your questions about who is The One for you. Let's take a look at the three assumptions that form the foundation for our approach:

1. *You do have a choice in the matter of love and attraction.* Contrary to the notion that we "fall" in love, or that somehow love overtakes us as though we have nothing to do with it, is the idea that we actively choose a partner to love.

2. *You are an agent of free will and you do have personal responsibility for the choices you make.* This notion holds each of us personally responsible for the choices we make in life, including our choice of a mate. Regardless of your background, history, or disposition, you are held accountable for your behavior in this arena.

3. *It is essential to know what you are looking for in a mate.* You should be highly discriminating in this matter because your choice contributes to your level of success or failure. Many people

assume that it doesn't really matter who you marry. They argue that what matters most is how you conduct yourselves and your level of commitment once married. This is not completely true. It is possible to make a very poor decision when selecting a mate and therefore suffer significant, if not irreparable, consequences.

This book is divided into three main sections: Looking for The One; Knowing When You've Found The One; and Choosing The One. Each chapter within these sections will include practical and realistic guidelines that will increase your opportunities for healthy mate selection. At the end of each chapter, there will be a section titled "The One Step You Must Take." This will challenge you to consider personal insights from each chapter, and it will encourage you to apply the truths you are learning to your life.

The person you choose to be your soul mate for life can potentially make you or break you. It's your choice! Get ready to discover the secrets to making this decision of a lifetime.

LOOKING FOR

The One

Chapter One

~

Your Quest
for The One

*L*eslie stands at the back of the foyer, nervously anticipating her turn to walk down the middle aisle of her home church. The pipe organ billows Pachelbel's Canon in D throughout the jam-packed sanctuary. She looks ahead to the front of the church where the apprehensive groom is standing. A few beads of sweat start to accumulate on his forehead as the bright lights shine down from above. Finally, it is Leslie's turn to march down the aisle, flowers in hand and custom-made dress fitted perfectly around her tanning-booth-bronzed body. Leslie begins walking to the cadence of the music, passing each pew neatly punctuated by candelabras. She approaches the front of the church, locks eyes with the pastor and winks at the groom, then takes a sharp left turn to assume that all-too-familiar position next to the other bridesmaids. Underneath her happy external façade lies a yearning to be at center stage. As she gazes over the congregation, she wonders to herself, *I'm attractive, I'm a fun person, and I love God. When is it going to be my turn? Will I ever find The One?*

If you are anything like Leslie, perhaps you can identify with feeling so close and yet so far. Maybe you have seen many of your friends get hitched and you are wondering when it will happen to you. Perhaps you have stood as the bridesmaid or groomsman for the umpteenth time and you are ready for your turn under the bright lights. Or possibly, you have broken up with someone you thought should have been The One, only to discover the person was definitely the wrong one. Still yet, some of you may have been previously married and you don't see any prospects for the future.

This book is for all those whose quest for The One has been elusive thus far. We will help normalize the quest and give you realistic guidelines to help dramatically improve your opportunities for achieving that ultimate goal. I (Ben) also personally played the role of groomsman far too many times before I finally tied the knot more than a decade ago. As I watched my friends take the plunge, one after another, shelling out who knows how much for rent-a-clothes, plane tickets, and groomsmen's and bridesmaids' gifts, I began to feel helpless in my quest for The One. Thinking back to this situation, I realized that there was one flaming catalyst for my angst—Pressure.

DO YOU FEEL THE PRESSURE
TO FIND THE ONE?

The Pressure to find that special someone hits us all sooner or later. Perhaps you can identify with The Pressure but you're not sure where it's coming from. I remember years ago in my mid- to late twenties wondering if I would ever find someone. My close friends had already found their mates and I had pictured myself also being married right out of college. What was wrong with me? At that time I felt pressure from many different angles. Let's take a look at the five different sources of pressure you may encounter:

(1) your family, (2) your married friends, (3) society, (4) your body, and (5) yourself.

1. FAMILY

It all begins with a phone call from your mom and her interrogating question: "Well, have you found anyone yet?" or the more subtle: "When are you going to settle down? I want grandchildren, you know." In spite of this well-meaning inquiry, it usually feels insensitive and burdensome. One way to respond to this intrusive interrogation is with quid pro quo. For instance, you might respond, "Well, Mom, I don't know. Have you dropped those extra thirty pounds yet?" This kind of counter-questioning usually puts a halt to familial pressure for a while (not to mention your good standing in the family will). Many times family members have expectations that don't fit your reality. They may even imply that singleness is unacceptable. What mom, dad, and most of your older relatives don't understand is that people are getting married much later these days for a multiplicity of reasons. In fact, almost half of the adult population is now single, compared to only 20 percent fifty years ago. For the majority, getting married in your early twenties is a thing of the past.

2. MARRIED FRIENDS

Don't you just hate it when your married friends seemingly rub their bliss in your face? Or worse, they are always trying to set you up with their friend with the "great personality"? Certain friends, basking in the glow of their recent marriage, often feel compelled to bring you up to their status instead of just letting you be. Actually, married friends can be a tremendous help to you in this process (see Chapter 3), but only after you have given them the proper coaching.

3. SOCIETY

Time magazine (August 2000) featured an article by Tamala Edwards titled "Flying Solo" in which she argues that more and more women are deciding that marriage is not inevitable and they can lead fulfilling lives as a single person. In spite of this trend, society and the media continue to portray the single lifestyle as a constant state of dissatisfaction. For example, many television shows, including *Friends, Ally McBeal, Sex and the City,* and others, are all about unhappy singles who are engaged in an endless spouse-hunt and yet can't seem to close the deal.

Likewise, the church adds fuel to the fire by making many students and singles feel like second-class citizens. Sadly, some churches have lost the ability to celebrate singleness and fail to recognize this state as a legitimate alternative within the Christian community. I received a letter not long ago from a singles pastor whose letterhead had this slogan: "Ministering to never married, divorced, and widowed singles." Wow, now that's a positive way to size things up.

> **Sadly, some churches have lost the ability to celebrate singleness and fail to recognize this state as a legitimate alternative within the Christian community.**

4. YOUR BODY

If you are in your mid-thirties, the ticktock of your biological clock can really turn up the heat in that search for The One. Additionally, there is the ever-present sexual "urge to merge" for those who are taking the high road by saving sex for marriage. Today, many women are adopting children or choosing pregnancy without husbands (à la Madonna) when they feel the right person is not to be found. Biological pressure to have kids or have sex is a strong, driving force in the quest for The One.

5. YOURSELF

From early childhood, most of us have been driven by an expectation that we will be married someday. There has always been an unspoken assumption that adulthood and marriage go hand in hand. Many people take this assumption for granted. Yet marriage is no longer the main rite of passage from adolescence to adulthood. When many of your friends are getting hitched and you feel stranded in the Dating Desert, it's easy to doubt yourself and put undue pressure upon your quest. Trust me, the other four pressure points are enough. But when you begin to compare yourself to your siblings, friends, and movie stars on the cover of *People* magazine who all seem to be happily married, you run the risk of catching a progressive

> Remember, marriage doesn't automatically make you an adult nor does it necessarily make you happy. Marriage simply makes you married!

case of self-pity. Remember, marriage doesn't automatically make you an adult nor does it necessarily make you happy. Marriage simply makes you married!

So, what do you do when The Pressure feels as if it is too much to handle? Eat ice cream? Take Prozac? Rent a Julia Roberts video? Some of those options would actually be better than the following list of desperate things we do when we let The Pressure get to us.

FIVE RECKLESS WAYS YOU RESPOND TO THE PRESSURE

1. PRESS THE PANIC BUTTON

We see couples young and old press the proverbial red panic button when their desire to have someone becomes uncontrollable. Panic-button daters will try to speed up the process of mate selection by picking up potential prospects in a chat room, taking out a desperate-sounding personal ad, hitting the club scene, or proposing within the first three months of a relationship. If you panic in your quest for The One, you could miss your true soul mate.

Mike and Randi met during their senior year in college. They were the reincarnation of Ken and Barbie—the model couple in every way. Although things looked great on the outside, on the inside both were extremely insecure and by no means ready to get married. After a whirlwind five-month courtship, they got hitched. Once they were married, well-hidden skeletons started coming out of the closet. Randi discovered that Mike had a drinking problem and Mike discovered that Randi was $70,000 in debt. Tragically, the couple never recovered from the Skeleton Shock Therapy treatment they used on each other, and their short-lived marriage was over.

2. SETTLE FOR MR. RIGHT NOW

I was stunned to read a recent magazine article suggesting that women should lower their standards for an acceptable mate. Too many people follow such unfortunate advice and compromise their standards. You want to choose The Right One, not just Mr. or Miss Right Now.

Janet is in her mid-thirties, highly intelligent, athletic, and deeply spiritual. She's been seeing William now for about seven months and it looks as if they may take the plunge. Janet has seen most of her friends get married over the past decade and her greatest fear is that she'll wind up single for the rest of her life. In fact, she's been waking up in the middle of the night in a cold sweat for weeks now because her friends and family have all expressed serious concerns about the relationship. William is nowhere near her league and she knows it. On a scale of 1 to 10, she's a 9, and he's only a 4 on a really good day. But it looks as though The Pressure is going to win out this time.

No doubt, some of you are way too picky and have a list that not even the Virgin Mary or Saint Peter could live up to, but don't swing to the opposite extreme of compromise when The Pressure gets to you. How do you know when you are starting to settle? Well, when you start to receive negative feedback from all the people who really care about you or you intentionally ignore obvious red flags, then you could be a prime candidate for compromise.

3. DENY YOUR HEART'S DESIRE

Another reckless way to respond to The Pressure is to deny your heart's desire to find a mate. Perhaps you have been deeply hurt in a relationship and you are afraid to love again; or you may just feel that your burning desire is wrong, so you deny that you want to find someone. However, to deny the built-in urge we have to be with a mate can be unhealthy. Some of you feel guilty right now because you have this intense longing. You've prayed that God would take it away and He hasn't. More than likely, God will not take it away because it represents a significant and valuable part of who you are.

4. CRAWL INTO A CAVE

Jonathan has given up the relationship ghost. He wants to meet The One. He's been in love twice, but hasn't gone on a real date since Reagan was president. In the past, he tried to meet people at church, the clubs, and the gym, and he even joined a dating service, but it never panned out. Now Jonathon fills his evenings with the new release movies from Blockbuster. He's quit the quest because the journey is too tough and too long. He has withdrawn into a dark, lonely cave.

Our hearts go out to Jonathan and folks like him who have simply given up. If you are the type that responds to The Pressure by retreating, let us encourage you to get back in the quest. Life is way too short and you have far too much to offer to stay in isolation. Perhaps this book will serve as a catalyst to get you engaged in life and back into the search.

5. SPIRITUALIZE YOUR QUEST

Many Christians take the superspiritual approach in their quest for a soul mate by expecting God to play the cosmic matchmaker or by trying to cut a deal with Him. Because some are afraid to take responsibility and make a real decision, they will

Many Christians take the superspiritual approach in their quest for a soul mate by expecting God to play the cosmic match-maker or by trying to cut a deal with Him.

look to God to confirm their quest through supernatural signs and leadings (Christianized versions of astrology and superstition). Some will use the "God told me you're the one I'm supposed to marry" line to get into a relationship and then have the nerve to turn around and use the "God told me we should break up" line to get out of the same relationship. (Now who do you suppose is confused here, God or you?) If God really does tell you who you are supposed to marry, then whatever you do, keep that to yourself and proceed as if you have heard nothing. Couples feed us this line all the time, falsely reasoning that if God tells them early in the relationship that this is The One, they can leapfrog over the normal, natural dating process.

If you're feeling The Pressure or you have become a little bit reckless in your search for the right person, take a look at the following four things you can do to depressurize your quest for a soul mate.

THINGS YOU CAN DO TO DEPRESSURIZE THE QUEST

1. FACE THE TRUTH

The first step you must take is to accept the reality of where you are and what you are feeling. This will require you to be open and honest with yourself. If you are yearning to be in a relationship, or feeling sad, alone, or frustrated, then be willing to face these feelings directly. The worst thing you can do is deny or internalize them. You must find a way to get these feelings outside of yourself. For example, you can talk to God about these longings, journal and write about them, or simply spend time talking to close, trusted friends. Regardless of the method you choose, it will help you to get these feelings, literally, outside of yourself. Whenever we try to deny what's going on in our hearts, we can damage our relationship with God, others, and ourselves. Often, we walk around with fake smiles plastered on our faces, when inside we are hurting and no one knows. It's important to admit the truth about what we are feeling and to include others in the process.

That is why we love the Psalms so much. The great psalmist, David, knew the importance of being genuine and expressing his heart to God. Consider what he wrote (in his journal):

> I am feeble and utterly crushed;
> > I groan in anguish of heart.
> All my longings lie open before you, O Lord;
> > my sighing is not hidden from you.
> My heart pounds, my strength fails me;
> > even the light has gone from my eyes.
> My friends and companions avoid me because of my wounds;
> > my neighbors stay far away. (Ps. 38:8–11)

Or:

> How long, O LORD? Will you forget me forever?
> How long will you hide your face from me?

How long must I wrestle with my thoughts
and every day have sorrow in my heart? (Ps. 13:1–2)

The best thing you can do to respond to The Pressure is to get honest. Pour it all out to God or a trusted friend, counselor, or pastor.

2. RELAX AND EMBRACE THE PROCESS

Once you've come to grips with how you really feel and what you desire, you can take a deep breath and relax. Allow yourself to embrace and even enjoy the process along the way. In fact, there is a strong correlation between your ability to relax during this process and your chances of finding a partner. Conversely, the more desperate or uptight you are, the more likely you will sabotage any potential relationships. Even if you do not outwardly display some kind of inner desperation, you run the risk of sending out this negative vibe anyway. Now, we're not saying you need to just "Let go and let God." No, it's not that easy, and a significant part of this book will teach you to be proactive in the dating process. In the meantime, we want to encourage you to "rest" and embrace the process for these reasons:

- God is more concerned about your love life than you are. If He cares about a sparrow falling from a tree, don't you think He cares about your romantic interests? We believe God is eager to join you in the quest and we want to help you discover a balanced view of His involvement.

- Maybe you haven't found The One because of timing. Not everyone gets married right out of college or in the twenties. Or perhaps you are not ready to meet The One at this point in your life. God may be working in you, on you, or through you in order to accomplish His greater purposes. You could be your own worst enemy. *You* may not be The One just yet. Or you could be engaged in some sort of self-sabotage and not even know it!

- You may be too young to be married anyway. If you are in high school or college, we're thrilled you are reading this book and we hope it will put you way ahead of the dating curve. Right now, you are learning how to relate to the opposite sex and still developing your sense of self and your identity. Your life will dramatically change between the ages of twenty-two and twenty-six, so don't be in a hurry to choose The One until you get a little farther down the road.

3. Never Compromise

It's not polite to curse. In fact, foul language is usually reserved for coaches and comedians on HBO who have a limited vocabulary. So, we want to add to your list of words that you should never use. The word is *compromise*. Whatever you do, wherever you go, you must not compromise in the quest for love. I'm reminded of Winston Churchill's famous line: "Never give in, never give in, never, never, never, never . . ." Just take that phrase and substitute the word *compromise*—Never compromise. Never, ever compromise. If you give in to The Pressure and compromise your standards on whom you date or whom you marry, you could suffer for the rest of your life. *It is far better to be single and lonely than married and miserable.*

We've talked to a myriad of people from coast to coast whose lives are shattered because they went against their gut instinct and made a poor marital decision. Far too many were content to jump into marriage with *anyone* rather than take the time to choose *The One*. Some of you are in a serious relationship right now and you are getting closer to engagement, but in your heart of hearts you know you are compromising on certain standards, or you simply do not have that soul-mate quality in your relationship. Do yourself and your partner a favor and walk away now (see Chapter 9, "Are You in Love with the Wrong One?").

4. CHANGE YOUR APPROACH

If you want to get results in your quest for The One, then you may need to change your approach. There's an old saying: "If you can't change the direction of the wind, adjust your sails." Well, in the dating game, you must be willing to look at yourself and consider whether or not you have some room for change. It's like working out. Let's say you have a goal to reshape your body and drop a few pounds. You cannot reach your goal if you eat junk food and avoid physical exercise (diet programs and pills don't work in the long run). Therefore, you have to change your old way of doing things. Basically, you start eating healthy foods and start some kind of aerobic activity. If you do this over a prolonged period of time, you will see results in your body and achieve your goal.

Apply that same philosophy to your love life. How can you get what you want if you're not open to changing your current dating strategy? Don't expect to get different results in your love life if you aren't willing to take action and change your strategy.

It never ceases to amaze us how helpless and passive some people are in their search for The One. It would seem that most would approach this all-important decision armed with skills, tools, and a strong sense of purpose. Your quest for a soul mate is no ordinary journey

> Your quest for a soul mate is no ordinary journey to be left to chance encounters and random associations. This is one of the most important decisions of your life.

to be left to chance encounters and random associations. This is one of the most important decisions of your life. Who you date and who you marry will affect every area of your existence—your career, your faith, your friends, your finances, and your emotional well-being. Yet so many people take the same old approach again and again, expecting to get new results. Are you open to new approaches? Are you willing to take responsibility for changing your strategy?

We will challenge the false assumption held by so many in our culture that finding a soul mate is some mystical process over which they have no control. Many people wait for something enchanting to happen in the heavens. Please, save that dream for Disney because finding The One does not have to be that complicated and otherworldly. This book is all about giving you earthy, realistic advice in your quest for a mate. If you are asking questions like these: "Is there only one person I can be happy with? Where can I find The One? What should I look for in a soul mate? How can I be sure this is The One? What are the signs this is not The One?" then read on and soak it in.

THE ONE STEP YOU MUST TAKE

After reading this chapter, can you identify with any of the pressures to be married? Are you capable of responding in reckless ways in your search for The One? If so, what specific action can you take and apply to your life in order to manage the quest? What steps can you apply to help you depressurize the quest? Use the space provided to write out your action plan.

_____

_____

_____

_____

_____

_____

_____

_____

_____

_____

Chapter Two

~

The Seven Myths
About The One

$\mathcal{A}$manda sat in my office with tears streaming down her cheeks. She was feeling a deep sense of grief as she contemplated a separation from her husband of six years. After a period of silence, she finally looked up and said, "I know that I married the wrong man; I must have missed God's best for me!" Amanda went on to explain how she had been told all her life that one special person was waiting out there, uniquely designed just for her. She recalled how her parents had prayed for "that young man" as long as she could remember, and how her enthusiastic grandmother had told her to trust God and that man would come along. She continued, "We have so many marital problems, there is no way this could be God's best for me. I'm not getting any younger, and if I'm ever going to find my true soul mate, then I need to start making some moves now." Sadly, Amanda had mistakenly assumed that her marital problems were the result of some grand mismatch; she believed that God had one special person in mind for her and that somehow she missed the cue six years ago.

My first meeting with Scott was rather intense. To say he was frustrated is an understatement. In fact, he was looking at frustration in the rearview mirror and rapidly approaching the realm of hopelessness. He began, "I'm desperate for answers. I've been searching since college and I still don't have a clue about finding

The One for me. I'm tired of hearing people tell me to wait for God's timing!" Scott went on to confess, "I'm thirty-five years old and still no one in sight! Is there something wrong? Something I should be doing?" Scott had asked some legitimate questions. He was fraught with confusion and despair and he needed some clear-cut answers.

DEMYSTIFYING THE MYTHS

Scott and Amanda have much in common. Their problems stem from various misguided beliefs—myths—about how people end up finding The One. Just like folklore, some of these beliefs have been handed down from one generation to the next, lasting so long they start to seem true. We know many of you are walking around with a suitcase full of these myths and you're not even aware of it. What is worse, these faulty beliefs can actually work against you in your efforts to find a loving, lasting relationship. We hope to expose these mythical assumptions, free you from their hindrances and barriers, and discuss the corresponding truths.

MYTH #1: THERE IS JUST ONE SPECIAL PERSON FOR YOU

Wouldn't it be nice, the notion that there is someone out there specifically designed just for you? Many people carry this hope that God, fate, or some other cosmic force has set apart someone for them. Additionally, this belief assumes that out of the six billion people walking the earth, there is but one true soul mate for you. Indeed, this notion is quite appealing and often hard to shake. There is tremendous security in the idea that the big matchmaker in the sky has already identified your mate and He will drop him or her off at your doorstep when you are presentable! It might feel very assuring to believe this is going on behind the scenes.

However, we believe that this kind of thinking can actually hurt your chances. For starters, this hyperspiritual approach is based upon unrealistic expectations about the way God works in our lives. It assumes a kind of deterministic philosophy (the idea of preselection, if you will). We believe that God delights in our ability to choose and exercise responsible judgment within the context of His greater will for all mankind. It's important to use common sense and good judgment in the dating process. Conversely, when we assume God has preselected someone for us, this can lead to a sort of passive and irresponsible approach to the process of mate selection. In short, it minimizes the need for common sense and it discounts the significance of human choice. When we understand that mate selection is our choice, it causes each of us to take personal responsibility for that choice once we're married. This enhances the commitment and provides a level of personal accountability. If and when marriage gets tough, you can't turn around and blame God or play the victim of fate. You are more inclined to say, "I trust that God led you into my life, I recognize there were good reasons why I chose you, and I take ownership of my choice."

MYTH #2: IF YOU LOVE GOD ENOUGH, HE WILL GIVE YOU A SOUL MATE

One of the most misinterpreted spiritual principles is taken from Psalm 37:4: "Delight yourself in the LORD and he will give you the desires of your heart." If taken the wrong way, this general principle can lead to a form of mechanical thinking about God. That is, praying hard enough, seeking His will long enough, and waiting patiently will guarantee a mate. Please understand, all these things are important and necessary but we cannot manipulate God into bringing us a partner. Some are guilty of approaching God as the big Santa Claus in the sky. If we are naughty, He punishes and withdraws His love or blessings from us. If we are nice, He will give us what we want. In the search for a life partner, this translates to: "If I am a good little Christian, God will bring me that special person; if I am bad, He will punish me and may withhold His best for me."

Do you remember Scott? He had bought in to this powerful myth. He made the assumption that he did not need to be responsible or proactive in his search for a life partner. He felt that it was more spiritual to delight himself in God, sit back, and then "wait" for God to deliver. In truth, Scott needed permission to take action. The goal is to balance personal responsibility with God's leading and timing.

What about you? Does your life or behavior suggest you are approaching God in a passive or superstitious manner? Rather than let go and let God, we would challenge you to trust God and get going!

MYTH #3: THERE IS ONE, TRUE CHRISTIAN WAY TO FIND YOUR MATE

Within the last decade, there has been a proliferation of Christian books claiming to be the one, true way to find your marriage partner. A common theme throughout is the idea that any form of modern dating is anti-Christian and unspiritual at best. For sake of simplicity we will refer to this as the "courtship model." In general, this model claims that God's way (or the biblical way) to find a mate is through a method of courtship where, through God's prompting, you identify a potential marriage partner before you ever spend intimate, one-on-one time with that person. Somehow, through God's direction, you come up with some vague assurance that this is The One before developing any kind of intimate friendship. You approach this person (and his or her parents) with your intentions to commit yourself to him or her with a view toward marriage! Does that sound a little scary?

In all seriousness, there are certainly some good principles in this model, including the emphasis on seeking God's guidance and involving the family in the process. Yet there are also many dangers, such as the tendency to overspiritualize your own selfish desires without truly examining your motives. This opens wide the door of manipulation in the name of God. Just as important, and more costly, is the temptation to try to shortcut a normal, necessary process of bonding that occurs through a long-term dating relationship. The courtship model seems to place the proverbial cart before the horse by creating an expectation for commitment way too soon.

> **The courtship model seems to place the proverbial cart before the horse by creating an expectation for commitment way too soon.**

By the way, the Bible does not stipulate any particular method of mate selection. It makes reference to mate selection according to the social customs of that time. (See "Biblical

Ways" graphic.) Specifically, it documents marriage by capture or by arrangement. The Bible does not model anything that even closely resembles courtship. Ironically, courtship is a type of free-choice mate selection that did not arise until the Renaissance, fourteen hundred years after the New Testament was written. So, the bottom line is that mate selection is a social construction, not handed to us from Mt. Sinai or taught by Jesus at the Sermon on the Mount. Dating is a fine and legitimate social practice, as is courtship (potentially), and people who practice either way should seek to do so in a manner that is respectful, responsible, conscientious, and in conformity with God's moral guidelines.

MYTH #4: FOLLOW YOUR HEART

This myth suggests that what really counts is how you feel in your heart. The emphasis is placed upon feelings and emotions. This is certainly one of the most widespread of the myths (reinforced by all kinds of media, especially Hollywood television shows and movies), and yet potentially the most damaging. This guideline for identifying a mate has absolutely no substance or practical application. It relies upon subjectivity and therefore discounts any objective basis for finding a partner. In Dr. James Dobson's book *Emotions: Can You Trust Them?*, he explains that emotions are often unreliable. He also concludes that while emotions can serve an important function, they are biased, whimsical, and at times, tyrannical. Certainly, when it comes to romance, our emotions are typically manipulated by hormones and they probably lie to us as often as they tell us the truth. The "follow your heart" approach could be influenced by something as superficial as indigestion or raw sexual energy. On the other hand, the

Top Ten "Biblical Ways" to Find a Mate

10. Find a prostitute and marry her. (Hos. 1:1–3)

9. Play Peeping Tom with the neighbor's bathing wife. Order her and have her delivered like pizza. (David, 2 Sam. 11)

8. Go to a party and hide. When the women come out to dance, grab one you like and carry her off to be your wife. (Benjamites, Judg. 21:19–25)

7. Find a man with 7 daughters, and impress him by watering his flock. You will get his daughter's hand in marriage for your trouble. (Moses, Ex. 2:16–21)

6. Even if no one is out there, just wander around a bit and you'll definitely find someone. It's all relative of course. (Cain, Gen. 4:16–17)

5. Become the emperor of a huge nation and hold a beauty contest. The winner is your wife. (Xerxes, Est. 2:3–4)

4. Agree to work 7 years in exchange for a woman's hand in marriage. Get tricked into marrying the wrong woman. Then work another 7 years for your bride. That's right, 14 years of toil for your wife. (Jacob, Gen. 29:14–30)

3. Purchase a piece of property and get a woman as part of the deal. Price includes tax, title, and license. (Boaz, Ruth 4:5–10)

2. Have God create a wife for you while you sleep. Note: this will cost you. (Adam, Gen. 2:19–24)

1. When you see someone you like, go home and tell your parents, "I have seen a woman; now get her for me." If your parents question your decision, simply say, "Get her; she's the one for me." (Samson, Judg. 14:1–3)

emotional draw could have deeper, unconscious roots related to unmet childhood needs. Even though a great number of people adhere to the "follow your heart" approach, this is a sure path to disaster. The road less traveled (yet more rewarding) requires you to balance both head and heart. There must be an intentional effort and decision to place common sense side by side with emotional appeal.

MYTH #5: DON'T WORRY, YOU'LL JUST KNOW!

I'll never forget my own struggles during my quest for The One. As my wife and I approached the more serious stage of our dating relationship and engagement became a real possibility, I started to experience doubts and some degree of ambivalence (I later found out this was normal). During this time I approached several married couples with questions about how I could be sure if this was The One for me. I remember getting the well-meaning but casual reply, "Oh, you'll just know." Others in leadership positions merely suggested, "Let it come naturally. It will all fall into place." Thanks for the tip!

Obviously they were trying to be encouraging, yet this kind of response had no particular practical value. I was looking for some clear direction, not some vague cliché. I had legitimate questions and needed some specific guidelines. I suspect most people are looking for the same. Unfortunately, the "you'll just know" cliché puts emphasis upon intuition and intellectual certainty. To be fair, there is probably a kernel of truth to this idea. At some point in the dating process, you eventually come to a place where you "just know." However, there are many important steps and guidelines that can help lead you to this point;

and we believe it is crucial to have an objective basis for identifying your mate. There are specific ways to assess levels of compatibility and tools to discern whether or not you are making a
wise choice.

The other disturbing element to this approach is the fact that
most people experience doubts throughout the dating process all
the way to their wedding day. This hesitancy doesn't necessarily
mean that the relationship is doomed. It may have nothing to do
with the health or stability of the relationship. In fact, we think it
is somewhat normal to experience a level of uncertainty even when
you meet the criteria that we will provide you in this book. It is
common for couples soon to be married to ask us, "How can you
know with 100 percent certainty if he or she is The One?" Our
answer is always the same: "You *won't* know for certain until you
walk back down the church aisle as husband and wife." Because ultimately, we all choose a partner based upon some measure of faith.
Again, it should not be "blind" faith, but a decision based upon a
balance of objective criteria, common sense, and subjective desire.

MYTH #6: ALL YOU NEED IS GOD

Jayne and Glen met at a wedding reception of a mutual friend
and seemed to hit it off immediately. They identified their love for
God and a passion for helping others. Each grew up in a denomination with "evangelical" in the name. Jayne had always been
enamored with South America, though she had never actually been
there. Glen was completing his final year in training for missions
work and had plans to go to Argentina for a stint. Aside from
those similarities, these two had nothing else in common! There
was a fourteen-year age gap between them, a lack of chemistry for

THE ONE

one of them, radical differences in their views on the priority of money, and significant differences of family backgrounds. Besides these few minor details, this was a "match made in heaven." When these two were challenged

> Unfortunately, in this day and age of rampant divorce (when the divorce rate is actually higher among evangelical Christians than the secular population) spiritual compatibility is not enough.

about their lack of compatibility in premarital counseling, they responded, "Yes, but we see eye to eye on the most important things (the spiritual matters) and we know God will smooth out the rough spots and cover over our differences." We firmly disagreed with this assessment.

Unfortunately, in this day and age of rampant divorce (when the divorce rate is actually higher among evangelical Christians than the secular population) spiritual compatibility is not enough. You must be able to connect on a number of levels. Compatibility should be broad-based, as will be discussed in the following chapters.

MYTH #7: THERE IS SOMEONE FOR EVERYONE

Our society puts a high premium on marriage, but for all the wrong reasons. Rather than elevating marriage because it is holy and sacred, some see it as the only real avenue for completion and wholeness. As a result, many people do not even consider "singlehood" a legitimate way of life. We believe that one of the major distortions floating around out there is that anything less than marriage is a concession.

Let's not mince words: marriage is not for everyone, and that's okay. We believe there are several types of people who probably should be single. Consider Jesus' words when asked about marriage:

> Not everyone is mature enough to live a married life. It requires a certain aptitude and grace. Marriage isn't for everyone. Some, from birth seemingly, never give marriage a thought. Others never get asked—or accepted. And some decide not to get married for kingdom reasons. But if you're capable of growing into the largeness of marriage, do it. (Matt. 19:11–12 *The Message*)

In other words, some have no real desire for married life. Consider Jesus, Paul, the pope, and Mother Teresa—we don't think they were incomplete because they were single. Who could argue that their lives were not meaningful and fulfilling simply because they were not married? Others might have a certain calling for a specific ministry. (And by the way, that doesn't necessarily mean God will take away their sexual urges and desires.) Still others may have a particular task in life that could not be accomplished if they were married. In the apostle Paul's first letter to the Corinthians, he placed heavy emphasis on the distractions of marriage and the benefits of being single. If you know people who are not candidates for

> Because we are individuals, our sense of wholeness and completion is something we embrace within ourselves in God through Christ. It is not dependent upon someone else.

marriage by choice or calling, then don't be afraid to affirm their decision. They need support, validation, and assurance that they are not "missing out."

Because we are individuals, our sense of wholeness and completion is something we embrace within ourselves in God through Christ. It is not dependent upon someone else. Second, it is possible to achieve intimacy without marriage or sex. David Webster, in his book *SoulCraft*, put it well when he wrote, "The longing of the soul is not for sex but for meaningful companionship." He goes on to explain that personal wholeness flows from our commitment to Christ—and nothing less will do! That's a truth you can take to the bank, and we encourage you to make this a reality in your own life, whether or not you ever get married.

THE TRUTH BEHIND THE MYTHS

These seven myths can significantly interfere with your ability to make wise choices in the dating arena. Even worse, they can potentially make or break a marriage relationship. Think back to Amanda's story. The lie she believed caused her to separate from her husband. Remember that she believed that she had missed God's best because of her marital struggles. Tragically, she is now divorced because she wouldn't let go of the illusion that God wanted her with someone else.

Scott had also believed the myths. He was sure God would eventually bring The One to his doorstep via first class mail if he would "seek God with all his heart" and just be patient enough! He got the first part right (seek God first) but he needed permission to get off his duff! Fortunately, he was able to realign some of his faulty assumptions. Scott is now married because he found a healthy balance between God's leading and his own personal responsibility.

 ## THE ONE STEP YOU MUST TAKE

Can you identify with any of these myths? Which ones seem to interfere the most with your quest for love? What is one step you can take to change your faulty beliefs and embrace the truth about your love life? Use the space provided to write down your action plan.

_____

_____

_____

_____

_____

_____

_____

_____

_____

_____

_____

Chapter Three

~

Where to Find
The One

$\mathscr{E}$veryone loves Tom Cruise. Women want to be with him. Men want to be like him. He's handsome, confident, charismatic, and worth millions. You may know him from the movies *Mission Impossible* and *Jerry Maguire,* but the movie that catapulted him to international stardom was *Top Gun.* Who can forget the scene when he walks into that club decked out in his navy uniform and Ray-Bans? After gazing around for a moment as if he owns the place, he turns to his flying buddy, "Goose," flashes a big smile, and says, "This is what I call a target-rich environment." (Translation: "The joint is packed with attractive, available women.") Moments later, "Maverick" (Cruise's character) grabs a microphone and winsomely serenades a shy Kelly McGillis with the classic love ballad "You've Lost That Loving Feeling."

Don't you wish finding The One was that easy? Wouldn't it be great if you had a target-rich environment in your city where you could go and meet plenty of eligible prospects? Guys, wouldn't you love to have the looks and moxie of a Tom Cruise? Ladies, don't you wish you could marry a Maverick?

Okay, enough fantasizing. Let's come down to earth and look at the cold, hard facts. If you are already in a relationship, then skip this chapter and save it for another day. But if you are available and in the quest, then by all means read on. Time after time, singles from all over the country and the world (we just got a letter from Spain with this very question) are asking us, "Where do I go to meet The One? I know what I'm looking for. I just don't know where to find him/her!"

Great question. Unless you believe that God is going to supernaturally bring The One to your doorstep, then you must take responsibility to place yourself in a Target-Rich Environment. This chapter will show you where successful couples are meeting these days and teach you how to create your own pool of potential dating prospects. We'll cover the whole gamut—from Internet chat rooms to mountain-climbing classes. Get ready to expand your playing field.

WHERE ARE SUCCESSFUL COUPLES MEETING?

We have surveyed well over a thousand engaged and married couples and asked them the simple question, "Where did you two meet?" We've concluded that most people meet at college, church, work, or through friends and family members. College has to be the most lucrative dating scene ever created. You are placed side by side for hours on end with people who are just like you in many ways. You have time to kill, chill, dream, and solve all the world's problems over a Domino's pizza. There are dances, clubs, study groups, parties, football games, and countless other opportunities to hang out. Sam and I met our sweethearts in college, though it took me several years after school to close the deal. But if your glory days are over, you need to be proactive to find a new place to meet dates. The good news is that most couples are now getting married after college, instead of the summer following graduation. Before we expand your dating horizons, let's look at the worst places to meet The One. Once you eliminate the less desirable locations, it will free you up to concentrate on the best places to meet available prospects.

THE WORST PLACES TO MEET THE ONE

BARS

Eric dove headfirst into the Atlanta nightclub scene the moment he arrived in the city. He frequented the most popular bars and clubs in town on a regular basis in his search for a soul mate. The love vibe was strong when he scoped out Monica for the first time, late one Thursday night. After a few dances, they headed for the local coffee shop to talk. It was love at first sight and the two began to hang out almost every night. Though both came from religious traditions that preached abstinence, they became sexually involved within the first three months of their relationship. After six months, Eric proposed to Monica and they married some time afterward. Once they were married, the sex rules changed and they had to start working on all the things they had ignored in their whirlwind courtship—things such as communication, forgiveness, finances, and affection. Sadly, their brief marriage is starting to unravel before their eyes and they realize how naïve and foolish they had been.

Let's face it—when the music is blaring so loudly that you can't hear yourself speak, and when the smoke is so thick that you have only about a foot and a half visibility, and when the alcohol you've ingested has transformed you into your alter ego, you're not in the right condition to meet a potential dating partner. Do people find each other in bars, get married, and stay together? Sure, but the odds are slim when you have all the noise, smoke, and personality-altering sub-

> Do people find each other in bars, get married, and stay together? Sure, but the odds are slim when you have all the noise, smoke, and personality-altering substances working against you.

stances working against you. If you desire to find Mr. or Miss Right, don't try the club scene. It is a waste of time, energy, and money, and at minimum is downright depressing.

DIFFERENT TIME ZONES

One of the most frequently asked questions we get at dating conferences is, "What do you think about long-distance relationships?" Our answer, "Not much." An MCI relationship is a setup for failure in your quest for The One. The focus in a normal dating relationship should be on getting to know someone. However, usually in a long-distance relationship the focus shifts from getting to know someone to getting to see someone. Granted, most people do not intentionally seek out an MCI relationship; it seems to just happen. Typically, these people meet each other on a trip or vacation, have an instant attraction, and then watch their phone bills quadruple in one month. MCI relationships are like attending a fantasy relationship camp. You talk on the phone incessantly, e-mail each other at work, and fly to various cities for a three-day romantic rendezvous. The problem is, you never really get the opportunity to see this person on a daily basis and deal with the reality of having someone in your face (and space) all the time. You can't possibly see the chinks in the armor when you are a thousand miles away. The only way you can determine if this is The One is to allow the letters MCI to stand for "Move Closer In." This allows you to see what your beloved is like on a day-to-day basis over an extended period of time. If you want the relationship to work, one of you is going to have to take the risk and move.

CHAT ROOMS

Thousands of singles around the world are finding steamy romances on the Internet. From sixth graders to serial killers, everyone has an equal opportunity to reinvent himself and find that special, virtual someone. To say that it's dangerous to meet people on the Web is a gross understatement. Recently, we did a radio show on the subject of finding love online and we were inundated with callers from around the country with horror stories that stretch the imagination.

Rochelle, a twenty-three-year-old, began an online relationship with Steven, a thirty-year-old lawyer from New York City. Rochelle lived in a tiny town outside of El Paso and became instantly infatuated with Steven's fast-paced and intriguing life. After a six-month cyber-relationship, she saved enough money to buy a plane ticket to the Big Apple to meet her Prince Charming face-to-face. After spending nearly seven hours trying to find his apartment, she finally succeeded and anxiously rang the doorbell. Much to her surprise, an older lady poked her head through the cracked door and asked what she wanted. Rochelle replied that she was there to meet Steven, a friend she had met in a chat room. The lady told her to wait, and moments later a fifteen-year-old boy appeared at the door. Rochelle was so crushed that she sprinted away from the apartment with tears streaming down her face. Too embarrassed to call and ask for money for the trip back home, she ended up living in a homeless shelter until she finally got up enough courage to phone a friend for help six months later.

Ted, a thirty-four-year-old from Mississippi, met a girl from Australia in a chat room. They e-mailed each other and chatted every spare moment, and Ted got the bright idea that he wanted to see her in person. So, he flew halfway around the world to meet his Web sweetie, but was shocked to discover his beloved had kept one little secret—she was six months pregnant. Minor detail.

If you think we are being too uptight about this one, then just hold on to your mouse. Since many of you will search the Web to find potential prospects anyway, we will give you some guidelines toward the end of this chapter to help make it safer, but for now mentally download the following reasons why you shouldn't go there:

- You never really know whom you are talking to.
- You put yourself at risk to be abused, robbed, or tricked.
- You say things you would never say in person.
- You tend to cultivate long-distance, dysfunctional relationships.

You may spend a thousand hours online together, but without face-to-face contact, you are literally strangers to each other.

Now that you have deleted these bad places to meet your soul mate, let's move on and look at the places where you are most likely to find a suitable match. These represent time-tested, Target-Rich Environments.

TARGET-RICH ENVIRONMENTS

CHURCH

Your local church is a great place to meet your mate. Nearly everyone I (Ben) dated, with one notable exception, I met at church. When you meet someone at church, the chances are much greater that you will share a common spiritual bond. There are many advantages of meeting someone in a religious environment. You already know this person either is seeking a relationship with God or has one already. Your views on morality and the sanctity of marriage will more likely be similar. Your circle of friends will also be similar. You will have a built-in support system with ministers and others who should encourage and train you in the process of building healthy relationships.

Don't fall into the trap of church hopping. Many single people are like little bees buzzing from one flower to the next and never landing in a particular church home. If you are always buzzing about, you will never stay long enough in one place to build deep friendships and you will never be a contributor to the work of God. One of the first questions I ask singles who are struggling in their love life is, "Are you plugged into a local church?" Too many times they are not, and hence they suffer from isolation and the "nobody loves me, everybody hates me" syndrome.

If you are not an active member of a local church, then get busy and find one. Look for a church with the following characteristics:

- A church that believes in the authority of the Bible and the divinity of Jesus Christ.
- A church that is Christ-centered and sensitive to the needs of students and single adults.
- A church where you can connect spiritually and socially.
- A church that encourages every member to get involved and serve others.

When you find a church that meets these criteria, then don't wait for a better deal. Make a commitment and join that church right away. Don't just warm the pew, but start asking other members how you can get involved and start serving others. God has designed you to live a life of service to others, because when you are solely looking out for number one, you will be miserable. The best way to prepare yourself for the Ultimate Unselfish Olympics (i.e., marriage) is roll up your sleeves and get busy serving others. When you are plugged in, as you will quickly discover, not only is it a great place to serve but it is also a Target-Rich-Environment.

WORK

We don't recommend fishing off the company pier to everyone because of the obvious inherent risks of experiencing sexual harassment suits or falling in love with your boss. However, according to a recent Fortune 500 survey, the workplace is rapidly becoming a dating hot spot.

One female investment banker put it this way: "The social scene is pretty dead now because AIDS and other worries have made people afraid of meeting strangers. Besides, who has time to go out?" Where did multibillionaire Bill Gates meet his bride? Try the marketing department at his company, Microsoft. People are working longer hours than ever before, so work has become a natural place to meet a potential mate. Most companies are taking a laid-back approach to office romances.

One big advantage of meeting someone at work is the possibility that you could have a similar background. Education, socioeconomic status, and life aspirations are just a sampling of common interests you may share with a coworker. The upside potential of finding love at work is tremendous, but so is the downside. Let's look at some basic "9 to 5" love rules.

> *Rule #1:* Make it a rule never to date someone you report to or someone who reports to you. This rule should be self-evident, but some people still don't get it.

> *Rule #2:* Consider the outcome if your relationship doesn't work out. Would you still have to see the person all the time and could you handle it? If an office romance goes sour, will that force you to find a new job?

> *Rule #3:* Don't ever pursue a relationship if it is not mutual. Getting slapped with a sexual harassment suit is no laughing matter.

FRIENDS AND FAMILY

According to surveys (our own and many others) we have consistently found that the vast majority of successful married couples meet their partners by networking through friends and family members. During my years in the Dating Desert, my close friends kept me from dying of thirst by continually introducing me to potential prospects and setting me up on blind dates. Some of the setups turned out well, while others were, ah well, not so good. In grad school, one of my married friends gave me a phone number of a girl he met at the library. I put the note in my pocket and didn't even look at it until later that night. I was stunned when I read the name. Unbeknownst to my friend, he had given me the phone number of my ex-girlfriend (and now my wife)! It was one of the few psychic moments in my life, not to mention a great excuse to give her a call.

Don't be afraid to ask your friends if they know of any available guys or gals. Chances are, if your friends connect with them, then you will probably connect with them as well. Be sure to coach your friends as to what you are and are not looking for in a mate. If you don't want them involved in this process, politely tell them so.

Believe it or not, family members can be a big help here. We tend to shun their advice when it comes to love, but often to our detriment. In reality, your family knows you better than anyone—the good, the bad, and the ugly. So, when they have a potential candidate for you, don't roll your eyes and brush them off too quickly. You could be missing out on a great opportunity.

Let's move from the traditional places of church, work, friends, and family and begin to color outside the lines.

DATING SERVICES

Many moons ago, I thought dating services were only for desperate people with absolutely no social skills. I was wrong.

More and more singles are bypassing the often laborious dating scene for these types of services. They offer complete confidentiality and the ability to sort through hundreds of potential dates before you ask one out. Some organizations specialize in setting you up for lunch dates only—a quick, safe way to meet potential dating prospects (not to mention a lot less expensive).

Before joining such an organization, check it out thoroughly. Some of them are about as trustworthy as used-car salesmen at the end of the month. Many are merely out to take advantage of your fears and prey upon your pocketbook. Others are solid organizations run with class, discretion, and professionalism.

PERSONAL ADS

I recently talked with a friend of mine who met his wife through a personal ad. They first had lunch at a very crowded restaurant and slowly proceeded down the path of love. They are both committed Christians and are now happily married to each other. When you write a personal ad, be sure to be discreet and honest. But above all, be safe. It's best to bring a friend with you when you meet the person for the first time, and always meet during daylight hours in a public place.

THE INTERNET

There's no doubt that the Internet is becoming the fastest-growing place to meet your mate, in spite of the inherent dangers. Since computers are all about speed, this form of connecting seems to share that same cyber-obsession for instant love. The Internet offers hundreds of different online venues to meet members of the opposite sex, from dating services and chat rooms to simple personal ads and high-dollar clubs. As we mentioned earlier in the chapter, this is not the ideal place (the chatroom approach being the worst), and at the very least you run the risk of entering into a virtual relationship without the benefits of a real relationship. However, we admit the fact that this isn't a moral issue and the jury is still out as to whether this is a legitimate place to meet potential partners; many of you may use the Internet anyway. So, if you dare to explore love online, then be sure to obey the following guidelines by America Online:

- Even though you may feel you've come to know that "special someone" through online interaction, DO remember that the people you meet online are, in fact, strangers.

- DON'T give out your phone number or address. Guard your personal information.

- DON'T believe everything you read. It's easy for someone to misguide you via online correspondence. Remember that the people at the other end may not be who they say they are.

- DON'T respond to any correspondence that is lewd or crude or in any way makes you feel uncomfortable.

- DON'T meet other members offline. If, however, you choose to meet someone, use good judgment and common sense. DO meet in a public place and in a group setting.

HOW TO CREATE YOUR OWN
TARGET-RICH ENVIRONMENT

EXPAND YOUR CIRCLE OF FRIENDS

A leading woman's magazine recently surveyed more than twenty thousand women concerning places and methods for meeting potential partners. Sixty percent acknowledged meeting their partners through a friend. Again, the obvious conclusion suggests the importance of having a wide range of friends for networking. Many times singles get caught in a social rut because they are not willing to broaden their friendship base. We talk with singles all the time who are content to maintain a "safe" distance from anyone new. Their entire social agenda consists of the same small group of people they see at church on Sunday morning and at Friday night softball. Please consider that you may have more to do with creating the circumstances for a relationship than you even realize. Many times people fail to take advantage of the opportunities that are right in front of them. It may be time to toss fate, luck, and chance out the window and begin the process of networking or placing yourself in the right environments.

Tim is constantly whining about his love life to me. He hasn't been in a relationship in years and rarely goes out. You would think by listening to him that he lives in Outer Mongolia, where dating is outlawed. But in

It may be time to toss fate, luck, and chance out the window and begin the process of networking or placing yourself in the right environments.

49

fact, Tim is a member of one of the largest churches in America, which boasts more than ten thousand single adults. He attends that church but is not involved in the singles ministry. I don't get it. That's like being a fisherman who has a pond stocked with Florida bass in his backyard, but is content to sit in his bathtub and bellyache over the fact that he hasn't caught any fish lately.

The first step to expanding your circle of friends is to be willing to get out of your comfort zone. For twenty-three years, I (Ben) only played the sport of basketball. Sometimes I felt more at home on home court than I did in my actual house. But several years ago someone turned me on to a new sport—two-on-two beach volleyball. I am now addicted to the sport and have met many new people as a result of stepping out of my comfort zone. I've been exposed to a whole new range of friendships I would have never known otherwise. In fact, some of my most intimate relationships have developed from being involved in this sport. If you are not willing to try something new, then the chances are that you will remain in your rut and forgo many opportunities to expand your friendships.

The next step is to take a personal inventory. What are your interests, hobbies, and passions in life? Select some of the interests and hobbies that you already have and take a deliberate step to meet more people who are into these same things. As you step out of the same, predictable, "safe" zone and get involved with the things you are passionate about . . . look around. You might be pleasantly surprised to see who's standing near you. If you need a jump start to add to your list of potential interests and places to meet someone, check out these suggestions:

- Take dancing lessons
- Join a running club
- Play on a softball, volleyball, or tennis team
- Try group rock-climbing
- Take a college course
- Volunteer at Habitat for Humanity
- Join a health club
- Take aerobics or spinning classes
- Join or start a book club
- Take cooking classes
- Enroll in foreign-language classes
- Participate in outdoor adventure clubs or singles cruises/vacations

 THE ONE STEP YOU MUST TAKE

Have you taken full responsibility to put yourself in a position where you can meet potential mates? Are you open to expanding your circle of friends? What is one step you can take to break out of your comfort zone and surround yourself with others? Use the space provided to write down your action plan.

_____

_____

THE ONE

_____

_____

_____

_____

_____

_____

_____

_____

_____

_____

_____

Chapter Four

~

Single for a Season or Single for a Reason?

$\mathcal{D}$o you wonder why you are still single?

Do you frequently fall in love and then break up before you get too close?

Do you have a habit of picking partners who are obviously wrong for you?

Do you fear that "all the good ones are already taken"?

Are you fed up with the boring, spineless, jellyfish types?

Do you suspect that there is just *no one* left for you?

Excuses. Blame. Rationalizations. It's fairly common to blame your surroundings, circumstances, and particularly, other people for your lack of success in the dating arena. And sometimes, as we have noted in Chapter 3, the problem is as basic as finding a Target-Rich Environment or surrounding yourself with the right people. However, the problem is often not outside of you, but inside. Sometimes the issue has nothing to do with location or the people around you. To illustrate, we can assume that you "live, move, and have your being" in a metropolitan or suburban context. By definition and sheer statistics, you are surrounded by numbers of people, all kinds of people; *and many are well qualified to be your soul mate.* Consider all the people you come in contact with on a weekly, if not daily, basis. Your path crosses people in your apartment complex or neighborhood, grocery store, bookstore, coffee house, workout facility, hike and bike trail, workplace, church groups, or 12-step groups, not to mention all the great opportunities such as social gatherings, clubs, and parties designed for the sole purpose of helping you connect with others. Furthermore, when you consider the world is getting smaller and smaller due to transportation and technological advances, that leaves a fairly large pool of possibilities.

Ironically, if you have any social life whatsoever, then finding a partner and falling in love shouldn't be all that difficult. People are everywhere and there are many potential "right ones" all over the place. In other words, The One is not some predesignated needle in the haystack set apart for you before the foundation of the world. From a statistical standpoint, you should be compatible and capable of connecting with hundreds of people. Yes, we said hundreds.

Now, we would bet that some of you are screaming out loud at us right now: "Where do you get off? Are you nuts? I'm always on the lookout and there is no one out there!" Unfortunately, the cold, hard truth is that your fears and insecurities may be keeping you from seeing the realities of love all around you. Or you are simply not ready to receive a partner and trust his or her love for you. For many, the tough part is getting beyond personal issues in order to identify and create a healthy, lasting partnership. In other words, the way to find your soul mate is to stop looking outwardly and take a look at yourself, inwardly. We are going to look at the four internal barriers that keep people from connecting with a soul mate, and the corresponding methods for overcoming these barriers.

INTERNAL BARRIERS TO FINDING THE ONE

Following is a list of internal barriers: things going on inside you that might be a hindrance to your search for The One. To reemphasize, we believe many people are already in the right environment, but are engaged in relational self-sabotage. People with these barriers will go to

> To reemphasize, we believe many people are already in the right environment, but are engaged in relational self-sabotage.

extraordinary lengths to obstruct the process. For example, they have an amazing ability to transform a guy who is tall, dark, and handsome into someone who is too tall, too dark, and just way too handsome. Others have a unique ability to pick partners who obviously have no real future potential. Still others can find a way to turn a perfectly good relationship into one that "just didn't work out." We want you to take the time to honestly evaluate where you stand on these issues.

1. Fear of Intimacy (Too-Close-for-Comfort Syndrome)

After working with a number of singles from all walks of life, we have come to discover some have a strong fear of intimacy that actually overrides their desire for relationship. Theirs is an ability to avoid having to know and be known. They put out a lot of energy in an effort to resist the very thing they are looking for. But let's get one thing clear. All of us fear intimacy on some level. It is normal and it is one of the tensions within all relationships.

57

Even in marriage, we want intimacy and closeness and yet we still fear it at the same time. What we are talking about here is the person who exhibits a *strong* fear that serves to sabotage potential relationships. (Note the emphasis on strong, which implies that we are talking about a matter of degree.)

Intimacy is about having the courage to be yourself in the presence of another. It is being able to do so with trust and to tolerate your partner's reactions. It's having the courage to be honest and real; to expose a balanced picture of who you really are, warts and all. You see, you can talk about yourself but never quite reveal your "real self." You can even share "deep stuff" but do so in a limited, guarded manner. In other words, you may have trouble exposing the more vulnerable parts of yourself. This fear of intimacy can also flow in the other direction. If you have a problem sharing your own world, you will certainly have a problem tolerating your partner's world. It is really quite simple. We all desire to be loved, accepted, and affirmed for who we are on the inside. But no one can provide these things unless we let the individual inside, to see us for who we really are.

Marla first came to see me with the primary complaint of being "unlucky in love." When asked about her situation, she confessed that for the past three years she had been fishing off the company pier, dating older men from work. One man was separated from his wife, another had children her age, and still another man (her boss) had made it clear from the get-go that this relationship was "just for fun." As we explored this pattern it became glaringly clear that she was attracted to "safe" relationships that had no real future. She could carry on for a while, knowing there was no possibility for real intimacy as long as she was with men who were ultimately "unavailable." Marla didn't wake up one morning and decide she would seek out these types. There was nothing intentional about her patterns. However, she finally took responsibility for her actions and admitted that her so-called bad luck was really about her fear of getting too close. This is just one of numerous examples where internal problems keep people from the real deal.

As we have discussed, the fear of intimacy is a universal and lifelong experience. Our concern is to what degree the fear of intimacy controls you. Take this test to determine if your fear of intimacy is obstructing your soul-mate connection:

IS YOUR FEAR OF INTIMACY TOO STRONG?

Do you fear losing yourself or your identity in relationships?

STRONGLY DISAGREE   DISAGREE   NEUTRAL   AGREE   STRONGLY AGREE

Do you have a long history of short-lived relationships?

STRONGLY DISAGREE   DISAGREE   NEUTRAL   AGREE   STRONGLY AGREE

Do you feel emotionally isolated, as though no one really knows you?

STRONGLY DISAGREE   DISAGREE   NEUTRAL   AGREE   STRONGLY AGREE

Does the mere thought of others knowing the weaker, needy parts of yourself feel intolerable?

STRONGLY DISAGREE   DISAGREE   NEUTRAL   AGREE   STRONGLY AGREE

Are you uncomfortable sharing your emotional and spiritual needs?

STRONGLY DISAGREE   DISAGREE   NEUTRAL   AGREE   STRONGLY AGREE

Is it difficult to allow others to support, love, and affirm you?

STRONGLY DISAGREE   DISAGREE   NEUTRAL   AGREE   STRONGLY AGREE

Do you experience a pattern of distrust or even paranoia when
you are in relationships?

STRONGLY DISAGREE   DISAGREE   NEUTRAL   AGREE   STRONGLY AGREE

Do you have a habit of picking partners that are obviously
wrong for you? (For example, people who are abusive,
unavailable, alcoholic)

STRONGLY DISAGREE   DISAGREE   NEUTRAL   AGREE   STRONGLY AGREE

Note: After taking this quick inventory, should you find that any of
your answers are *Agree* or *Strongly Agree*, we suggest you take action to
address your concerns (see "Tips for Overcoming the Barriers" toward
the end of this chapter).

2. FEAR OF REJECTION (PLAY-IT-SAFE SYNDROME)

The fear of rejection is closely linked to the fear of intimacy
because both value safety and protection from hurt. In fact, one
often leads to the other. Understand that rejection is always a possibility; it's just part of the package when attempting to establish a
relationship with someone. Love always includes vulnerability to
rejection or loss. We've yet to meet someone who found a way to
enter a relationship risk-free, no matter who he or she is. As C. S.
Lewis once stated, "The only place you can go and *not* experience
rejection is a cave or a cemetery." Sometimes your fear of rejection
can cause you to play it too safe, drastically narrowing your opportunities for finding the right partner. Have you come to terms
with the rejection factor? If not, we recommend you accept the
reality of rejection. Now obviously, the stronger you are on the
inside, the less threatening this reality will be. We emphasize this

in the first chapter of our book *The Ten Commandments of Dating*. Commandment One, Thou Shalt Get A Life, suggests that when you have a solid identity and you are in touch with your intrinsic worth and value, you will not be shaken or destroyed by rejection.

3. FEAR OF EQUALITY (THE ONE UP/ONE DOWN SYNDROME)

Anna was a twenty-eight-year-old who was struggling to find a partner. She was attractive, had a charming personality, and had a capacity for depth. But oddly enough, there was never anyone who seemed to be right for her. She was active and involved socially, but never quite "hit it off" with anyone. She was rarely asked to go out and thus concluded, "There just isn't anyone out there for me." Now that's a bold statement. You mean there is literally *no one?* We find that impossible to believe. Can you identify with some of the other lines falling into this category: "All the good ones are already taken" or "I can't find anyone who is even close to what I'm looking for" or "No one will ever love me"? If you find yourself making these kinds of statements, then you have much in common with Anna.

When people make these extreme assertions, they haven't come to terms with the reality of equality. We refer to this as the "one up/one down syndrome." That is to say, some feel that they are either too good for everyone (superior, or one up) or not good enough for anyone else (inferior, or one down). In either case, this represents a skewed perception of self and others and defies reality. One way or another, we must understand that as humans we are much more alike than we are different. The key is to begin to see yourself more realistically, which is to say you need to see yourself and others the way God sees you. You are a child of God—a special creation with infinite worth and value. So are those around you! The exciting thing is that once you realign your perceptions and come to terms with this truth, a vast group of people will spring forth as more similar than different. Consequently, people you once felt were "one up" become more accessible friends. Likewise, people whom you saw as "one down" all of a sudden become much more desirable.

By the way, as long as you see others as so vastly different (inferior or superior), then you don't have to face the vulnerability that comes with true closeness and intimacy (there's that word again). It's just another convenient way to keep a safe distance from others.

4. FEAR OF COMMITMENT (BEST-OF-BOTH-WORLDS SYNDROME)

Last, we tackle the fear of commitment. This is probably the most frequently discussed reason for not making a connection. A commitment-phobe is simply not yet ready for a serious, long-term relationship. He enjoys his singleness and the freedoms that come with it. (While we recognize that this can affect either gender, it is more prominently a male "disorder.") It's not that he doesn't crave a companion; he does. The problem is that he wants the best of both worlds: the relationship without the commitment. It is really more about ambivalence—the inability to choose one over the other. He feels stuck in the middle and almost paralyzed by indecision. In the most extreme cases, he is a perfectionist, and his fear of making the wrong decision (and we concede this is a big one) prevents him from making any decision at all. Or perhaps he wants a partner but he doesn't want to make the sacrifice. He wants companionship without any strings attached. Maybe he won't commit because of his unrealistic expectations. He doesn't understand the difficulties and challenges that come with all relationships. Could this be you? Might you have some ambivalence about staying in a committed relationship? Are you willing to address the difficulties and challenges inherent in relationships?

All of these fears are real—fears of intimacy and rejection or fears of equality and commitment. And they don't just come out of nowhere. They come from deep within, as a result of your relationship history. Usually, you will find a key figure from your past who contributed to some deep hurt or feelings of rejection. However, these fears do not need to have so much power over you. You can choose to do something about them, starting today, although it will take intentional effort and a real commitment on your part. In fact, if you have taken an honest self-inventory and acknowledged a significant fear within you, then you are already halfway home in terms of overcoming this barrier in your life.

If you aren't sure whether one of these fears is affecting your search for The One, get two or three people you trust to help you assess yourself. Ask them point-blank: "Do I seem to have a fear of intimacy, rejection, equality, or commitment?" Then listen carefully to what they say. You may need their objective feedback in order to complete your assessment. In addition, we suggest you follow the tips we offer here.

TIPS FOR OVERCOMING THE BARRIERS

FACE YOUR FEARS HEAD-ON

The more you give in to your fears, the more power they can have over you. When you avoid situations that you fear, such as close, intimate relationships, you simply make the problem worse—that's a guarantee! Conversely, when you take action and "do" the very thing you fear, the less fear you will have. Consider that having courage means doing something despite your fears. Be courageous, acknowledge your fear, and then do whatever it is you have to do.

GET INTO SAFE RELATIONSHIPS

You cannot work on relationships unless you are in them. Step out. Take a risk and allow yourself the freedom to be in relationships in spite of the vulnerability this may create. But don't just get into any relationship; be wise and discerning about surrounding yourself with safe people. Make sure you find people with character and integrity who can love, affirm, and support you. When you get out of your comfort zone, by definition, it will feel uncomfortable. But that's okay because the discomfort of overcoming your fears is well worth the reward of intimacy and companionship that follows.

LEARN HEALTHY SELF-TALK

Pay attention to your inner dialogue. What are you saying to yourself about relationships and the fears you may have? Is your self-talk negative, hopeless, pessimistic, or unrealistic? For example,

Suzanne grew up with a critical mother who had the gift of seeing the negative in every situation. As an adult, Suzanne has been "blessed" with the same gift and constantly finds herself saying things like, "This relationship will never work out" or "I'll probably get burned" or "He wouldn't love me if he really knew me." The good news is that Suzanne has the power and ability to change the way she thinks, which in turn will affect how she feels about herself and the image she projects to others. You, too, can change your distorted thinking. Start filling your mind and heart with positive, hopeful statements and create a healthy, self-fulfilling prophecy.

SEEK PROFESSIONAL HELP

Sometimes our insecurities and fears are so deeply rooted that we have to seek out professional help in order to address them effectively. Don't hesitate to invest in a process of counseling or therapy to increase your self-awareness and your potential for personal growth. We are always amazed that people will spend thousands of dollars on automobiles, fashion, and entertainment, but refuse to spend a dime on their own personal growth in order to improve their relationships with God, self, and others. In fairness, we recognize that most people use money as an excuse and the real issue is about having the courage to do something that could be life-altering. Remember, as creatures of habit and comfort, we all resist change; yet growth requires change. Here's a thought: the average person spends eight hundred dollars at Starbucks per year. For that kind of money, you can begin to develop a new identity and kick the caffeine habit all at the same time.

THE ONE STEP YOU MUST TAKE

Do you identify with any of the internal barriers? Have you been challenged by the idea that you could be your own worst enemy in the dating game? If so, what is the one practical step you can take to begin to address your fears head-on?

_____

_____

_____

_____

_____

_____

_____

_____

_____

_____

_____

_____

KNOWING WHEN YOU'VE FOUND

Chapter Five

~

The Love Target

$\mathscr{S}$tarbucks has become a cultural phenomenon and certainly one of the most popular social venues of the new millennium. The company has mastered the art of charging exorbitant prices and somehow making you feel good about it (the managers even put out a tip jar!). Here you can meet new people, gather with friends, or just have a relaxing time over a cup of coffee without doing anything illegal, immoral, or unethical.

A while ago, we were hanging out at our local Starbucks together discussing an outline for this book and nursing a $5 venti-traditional-half-caf-quad-vanilla-nonfat-mocha latte. It was comforting to know that 5 percent of the proceeds were going toward preservation of some remote rain forest in South America. Anyway, during our discussion we began throwing around words like *the one* and *soul mate*.

Eventually, we noticed there were several people eavesdropping on our conversation. So we invited them to join in. Three women in particular caught our attention. The first woman, Amy, was divorced after six months of marriage. According to her, she had based her decision to marry on pure, raw passion. (She called it "mutual sexual energy.") She indicated that much to her surprise her ex-husband was now running around with younger and more energetic women. The second woman, Vivian, was still married after ten years but sadly felt she had not married her soul mate. Her basis for marriage was fairly sound, as she felt compatible in many areas except one—they lacked spiritual compatibility. Vivian properly concluded that their level of intimacy could only go so far because of this essential area of incompatibility.

The third woman in this group, Wendy, was happily married to the man she considers her "best friend." The difference between these three women was that Wendy was successful in marriage simply because she chose wisely. She said, "I married my best friend. We grew up together and we just fit naturally." As we continued to explore her basis for marriage, we discovered she married her soul mate because they connected on many levels, including the spiritual dimension. Interestingly enough, Wendy represents a perfect example of someone who connects with her partner in the three essential "love" zones: relational compatibility, character, and spirituality. These three zones make up what we call the Love Target. Now, Wendy did not explicitly create a Love Target in her quest for The One, but she found a lasting, soulmate relationship because of her connection in these three essential areas. Let's take a look at the three zones and the components that form the Love Target.

THE LOVE TARGET

When we first began to discuss the concept of the Love Target, I'll never forget one Friday morning on my drive to the office, I found myself humming along with the song on the radio. The chorus of this Backstreet Boys' number one hit echoed: "I don't care who you are, where you've been, or what you've done, as long as you love me."

What!? I thought. *You mean it doesn't matter who your girl-friend is? What if she is the founder of some New Age cult? You mean it's okay that your boyfriend is a pathologically lying, two-timing, back-stabbing gigolo?* It suddenly occurred to me that this was the antithesis of everything we would write about finding your soul mate; but unfortunately, these words reflect what many people believe to be true. This song suggests that a specific target or criterion is irrelevant in your search for The One. According to this number one ballad, issues such as compatibility and character are not important. Don't be discriminating about your mate because all that really matters is that you find someone who happens to love you! It's this kind of mentality in our culture that we are up against, and we invite you to consider a better way.

The Love Target is a model or paradigm that we have developed to give you the criteria and help you organize your priorities in selecting a soul mate. This target is arranged in three concentric circles representing the three essential elements (love zones). It is based upon the premise that your ideal soul-mate relationship can be attained only when you connect with your partner in all three love zones:

- The Relational Zone (Relational Compatibility)

- The Character Zone (Essential Character Qualities)

- The Spiritual Zone (Core)

The order is important because each zone symbolically represents an increasing need for discernment and, hence, time. (We just can't say that enough, but we will keep trying.) For example, the outer zone of the Love Target (Relational Compatibility) includes general attributes and qualities about a person that are more obvious and easily discernable because they are external ("outer") characteristics. This outer zone includes such characteristics as physical attraction, personality style, and lifestyle. In general, we are initially attracted to someone for the more obvious qualities, such as looks or personality, but we should continue a relationship over time based on connection in the inner zones.

The middle zone of the Love Target (Essential Character Qualities) consists of qualities that lie beneath the surface. By definition, these attributes are more difficult to observe and include such qualities as honesty, faithfulness, loyalty, commitment, forgiveness, self-control, discipline, endurance, and the like. These qualities can be discerned only with some degree of intention over a long period of time through a variety of circumstances arising over the normal course of life. This bears repeating: these qualities are discerned over

> You cannot identify essential character qualities in the first three months of a relationship.

a *long period of time.* You cannot identify essential character qualities in the first three months of a relationship.

Finally, the inner zone of the Love Target (Core) represents the essence of who you are and comprises your theology, beliefs, values, and sense of purpose and meaning in life. It is only through connection in this arena (along with the other zones) that your deepest longings can be fulfilled in another person. Furthermore, all of one's attributes and behaviors seem to flow out of this inner core. As would be expected, this innermost part is going to be the most difficult aspect to identify in another. However, it will also be the most critical connection in a long-term relationship. It will require time, patience, and a keen sense of perception, as will be discussed in the following chapters.

Some might say, "Wait! I've known my partner only a short time, and we have already discussed our beliefs. It's amazing! We have deep conversations about spiritual issues and values and we think the same! See, it doesn't take a lot of time to get to know the Core." Not so fast. As the relationship police, we have to issue you a warning. In our experience, *often* it is the very men and women who get vulnerable early on and "share" their deepest beliefs with you who are the ones least to be trusted. They know that disclosing this level of depth has the effect of creating intimacy. Thus, they can appear to share their core, when in reality they are just doing an Oscar-winning performance with the right lines. We have talked with countless women (and some men) who feel confused and betrayed because they thought they knew a person's core and found instead a wolf in sheep's clothing. Others were disillusioned when they discovered their early intimacy did not equal mutual commitment. Knowing both the character and the spiritual zones of another person takes time. There is no substitute for time. None. When people are not committed to take the time to connect in all three love zones, they are following the ways of the world—*they're living in sin!*

ARE YOU SINNING?

The word *sin* is the English translation of the Greek word *hamartia*, which literally means "to miss the mark." The New Testament was originally written in Greek and the word *hamartia* was a term originally taken from the sport of archery. When an archer was out practicing his aim, if he did not hit the bull's-eye, the judge would raise a flag and yell out "sin" to convey that the archer missed the mark. In working with numerous engaged couples, we have often been tempted to throw a flag and shout out "sin" when we encounter gross negligence because they have missed the mark of true compatibility. Anytime you fail to hit the bull's-eye of the Love Target, you are compromising and settling for less.

> **Anytime you fail to hit the bull's-eye of the Love Target, you are compromising and settling for less.**

PLAYMATE, INMATE, OR SOUL MATE?

We have used the Love Target with many couples and individuals to help them in finding a true soul mate. And to be perfectly honest, some have taken our advice and committed only to marry someone who fits in all three zones. Others have ignored our direction and married based upon partial compatibility only to discover the devastating consequences of their compromise too late.

Many people aim only for the outer edge of the target (relational compatibility). They assume they have met a soul mate because they have the chemistry and perhaps a lot in common (they have jobs, drive cars, like movies, and breathe in and out), but that is just not enough. They may have found a *playmate*, but certainly not a soul mate.

Remember Amy from Starbucks? She had found a playmate; someone who could share pleasure, fun, and laughter. She later implied her aim was haphazard at best—and the result: she "missed the mark." Vivian was closer, as she connected in two of the three zones but still missed the bull's-eye. When marriage gets tough and the inevitable storms of life hit, she and her husband have no spiritual base to share. Since Vivian and her husband do not share a common religion, and hence morality, they have no common foundation from which to make life decisions. She longs for the day when she can pray with her husband or just share her soul without being ridiculed. Oh, sure she will stay married and raise her kids, but deep down there is an ache for something more. She feels trapped and imprisoned. She longs for a soul mate but she has become an *inmate*. The good news is that you don't have to experience the longing and regret that come with missing the mark. You can do better than a playmate or an inmate. When you have a clearly identified target and your aim is sure, you are well on your way to finding the kind of relationship with a soul-mate quality.

HOW'S YOUR AIM?

In the game of love—as in life—you are likely to hit whatever it is you are aiming for. If your aim is haphazard, you will hit a random target—whatever happens to fly by at the time. If your aim is sure but misguided, you will hit the wrong target and end up with someone who is not right for you. This is precisely what plagues those well-meaning individuals with the wrong target in their sights.

> In the game of love—as in life—you are likely to hit whatever it is you are aiming for. If your aim is haphazard, you will hit a random target—whatever happens to fly by at the time.

All successful endeavors (including marriage) are based upon a clear vision of what is to be accomplished. You must have a clear picture of the goal in order to achieve the results you expect. Or in the wise words of Stephen Covey, author of *The Seven Habits of Highly Effective People*, we must "begin with the end in mind." This principle holds true for everything from a major military campaign down to an insignificant trip to the grocery store. Regardless of your goal, you want to have a clear picture of your mission. In order to accurately picture the goal of finding a soul mate you must have a good understanding about what you value and what is most important to make a successful choice. So you need a specific goal, a target for which you are aiming. This specific goal is what we are constructing in your personal love target.

CONSTRUCTING YOUR LOVE TARGET

Your love target is not something you identify overnight. It will require careful self-analysis and serious introspection over a period of time as you consider the things you most value in a future partner. It is a bit like putting together a mission statement. Successful organizations spend a great deal of time hammering out a mission statement that guides everything they do. Successful athletic teams fix a goal in mind and then execute every practice and game in light of that goal. Covey also argues that "all things are created twice." He explains that there is a mental (or first) creation and then there is the physical (or second) creation. For example, in order to build a house you design every detail on paper before you ever break ground or hammer a nail. You work with your mind in order to get a clear image of what you want to build. Likewise, in your quest for a soul mate, it is crucial to use your imagination first to visualize what you need and who would meet those qualifications. We know this seems obvious, yet the overwhelming majority of people do not take the time to identify and specifically write down what they need in a mate.

In the next three chapters, we provide guidelines and categories to aid in the process of constructing your own mission statement (your love target), but you will make the statement for yourself. We will give you the general structure so you may custom-design the mission to fit your values, needs, and priorities. Keep in mind that some people already have an unconscious love target. They are driven by an unexamined vision or an unspoken ideal. And in the hunt for love, this is where a lack of intention and proactivity gets people in trouble. You must be clear about what is really driving you in your quest for a soul mate.

Chapter Six

~

Your Relational Zone

*S*andy and I had been waiting for her fiancé, Rex, for more than twenty minutes in my office when he finally bolted through the waiting room door. The moment I laid eyes on Rex, my "sharp" clinical skills kicked in gear and I instinctively knew something was amiss. Rex had on a white jumpsuit, soaked in sweat and stained with mud and grass. He was in the lawn service business this month. Sandy, on the other hand, was wearing a tailor-made navy blue business suit (standard issue at her Fortune 500 firm). Rex finally mumbled an apology for being late and reluctantly sat down to join us for our first premarital counseling session together. As we proceeded through the standard Q & A, it didn't take Sigmund Freud to figure out what was going on here (so much for my sharp clinical skills).

How can I put this delicately? Rex was a simple guy with little inclination for high society (translation: in her eyes he would always be underdressed, unshaven, unmotivated, and possibly unemployed). On the other hand, Sandy was refined and highly cultured (translation: she would always be high dollar, high society, and high maintenance). Toward the end of our session, Sandy stated with glee, "Rex is one of the most handsome men I've ever known; he looks so much like my *father*, but there are some things I'm concerned about." That provided the perfect opportunity for me to suggest they postpone their upcoming wedding and let us continue to explore some issues before they decide to tie the knot. Fortunately, this couple paid attention and took my advice this time (it's not always that smooth). You see, even though Rex and Sandy were both Christians and they were "in love," they were simply incompatible (on a myriad of levels). Tragically, these two people would have been prime candidates for the most frequently cited reason for divorce in our country—mutual incompatibility. They had little in common. They were out of sync in too many areas including background, education, personality, priorities, interests, and the manner in which they approached the world.

Like many mismatched couples, a relationship that lacks natural harmony is like the chaotic sound of an orchestra tuning up before a performance, when each musician is making his own noise. The dissonance and disunity are enough to make your skin crawl. But at the symphony, once the performance begins, the conductor unifies the musicians and creates beautiful harmony. Unfortunately, there is no such thing as the relational conductor who can just wave his baton and create harmonious relationships out of chaos. The simple truth is that a good, healthy relationship must generally start off with a sense of harmony and rhythm. When two people begin to join their lives together in a dating relationship, it should not have

> When two people begin to join their lives together in a dating relationship, it should not have to be forced or contrived; there should be many similarities and a natural connection.

to be forced or contrived; there should be many similarities and a natural connection. In this chapter we will give you direction to help you determine the crucial components of relational compatibility.

THE
RELATIONAL TARGET

HOW TO KNOW IF YOU ARE
RELATIONALLY COMPATIBLE

The Relational Compatibility Zone comprises those outer characteristics or qualities that can be identified in the beginning stage of a relationship. As mentioned, these are the more obvious qualities that should be evident within the first four to six months, before a relationship gets too serious. (There's that idea of time again. Do we need to issue another speed warning?) If you have been dating someone for less than four months, it should not be too serious yet. For the sake of simplicity, we have broken this down into three different categories:

1. Chemistry (Physical and Emotional Attraction)

2. Personality style

3. Lifestyle (Interests and Hobbies)

As we discuss these three components, take note of the importance of having each of these as an intrinsic part of your current or future relationship.

1. CHEMISTRY

There are many aspects of a relationship that you can create, nurture, and even develop over time. This isn't one of them. Let's just say from the outset that chemistry is the most mysterious of all the components. It represents a mixture of multiple factors including looks, personality, sense of humor, speech, vibe, spirituality, and more. As such, there are no easy three-step formulas for developing chemistry. Often there is no rhyme or reason to this element; either you have it or you don't! You can't conjure it up from the depths or force it into being. Rather, it should be natural and instinctual.

To be fair, men and women differ somewhat in this area. Research supports what we already know intuitively: that there are significant gender differences in the qualities sought in mate selection. As an example, women are more selective in terms of seeking emotional security and financial stability. On the other hand, men are more selective (or should we say shallow?) in terms of attraction, and more interested in qualities such as physical appearance and stamina. Let's take a look at the general differences.*

WHAT MEN ARE LOOKING FOR

Although this is a broad generalization, men are *initially* attracted to what they see on the outside. In general, men are drawn to women by qualities that are more physical in nature: someone who is lively, healthy, attractive, and youthful, to name a few. Fifteen years ago, I (Sam) walked into a room and spotted a heavenly creature. She was, without a doubt, the prettiest woman in existence. She was clothed in dazzling white and surrounded by brilliant lights; I even heard heavenly music playing in the background. Okay, I saw her in church and she was wearing a white sundress and sitting next to the window on a very sunny July afternoon. Nonetheless, there was something awesome and compelling about this angel, so I went closer and sat down next to her. For me, this was the initial spark—the attraction was immediate, irresistible, even primitive. Little did I know at that time that we would be married three years later (it took longer to talk her into it than I thought). Of course, in time I discovered that my wife had many great qualities that I came to appreciate as much as her outer beauty, but it was her initial presentation that ignited the flame of attraction and drove me to

---

*Authors' Disclaimer (as required by attorneys): We don't make the news; we just report it! We're not saying this is how it should be or how we want it to be, but let's face it—it is what it is. At least for the majority. Remember, we're just the messengers.

know her even more. This is what chemistry and attraction sometimes look like from a man's perspective. The nature of attraction is such that it is compelling—it draws you in like a magnet.

To put this in perspective, let us state the obvious: the female body is an incredible work of art, a masterpiece crafted by God Himself, while the male body is generally hairy, lumpy, and should never be seen in the light of day! Most men can appreciate this reality. Subsequently, a woman's physical attractiveness is all about what she does with what she has, simply that she takes good care of herself and presents herself well. It is making the most of her unique God-given characteristics. It has nothing to do with trying to conform to some objective standard or criteria like the *Vogue* supermodels—they're much too skinny anyway, right?

If you are serious about developing a relationship with a man, then you need to be willing to explore your attractiveness. For example, identify your best features and show them off! Accentuate your eyes, smile, hair, or whatever is your loveliest asset. It's not unspiritual to get a makeover, experiment with a new hairstyle, or try out a new style of clothing. Second, being "youthful" or "healthy" is not at all related to your age. It has more to do with your attitude and lifestyle. Being physically fit and healthconscious and pursuing life with passion are part

> The female body is an incredible work of art, a masterpiece crafted by God Himself, while the male body is generally hairy, lumpy, and should never be seen in the light of day!

of creating an attraction. You automatically increase your attractiveness when you exude an attitude of vibrancy, zest, and enthusiasm. Remember that beauty is in the eye of the beholder. All men are uniquely wired and vary as much in the qualities they are attracted to as the many sports teams they cheer for. Don't try to be something you're not, but be the best you that you can. Be yourself. It's a hard act to follow.

THE ONE DANGEROUS ATTITUDE: JUST AS I AM

Some women have a tendency to believe that "no man is worth attracting if he cannot accept me just as I am!" This attitude suggests that it is okay to disregard outward appearance because "a good man should be able to accept me and love me for who I am on the inside." In an ultimate sense this is true. First Peter 3 instructs that a woman's beauty should come not from outward appearance, but from the inner self, the unfading beauty of a gentle and quiet spirit. However, we are talking about *initial* attraction. There is nothing inherently wrong with beauty and charm, although at times they can be misused to deceive and manipulate. Hanging on to the "just as I am" rationalization can surely interfere with meeting the man of your dreams because he will never be able to see past the initial presentation. Women who do not take care of their health or who are unwilling to present themselves attractively are illegitimately raising the bar of their expectations of men. They are demanding that men, during a first-time encounter, ignore part of their male, God-given senses and see right into their pure hearts or priceless souls. This is a very idealistic and, incidentally, impossible task. It all depends on whether you want to get married in the real world or the imaginary world. In the real world men are often attracted initially to your appearance. Even preachers and missionaries. You would fare much better to present yourself well and enjoy the pursuit of men who are attracted initially and thus want to get to know you better.

WHAT WOMEN ARE LOOKING FOR

For women, the attraction is a mixture of the physical and emotional (a little bit physical and a whole lot emotional). Women are primarily interested in two things: protection and security. They will be drawn to a man who can provide for them a sense of safety as well as financial, physical, and emotional security (and guys, it's much less financial than you think). In other words, physical attraction for women represents a small part of attraction; it is secondary at best. Feeling a sense of security (relationally, emotionally, and financially), safety, and stability—these are the things that account for that spark for women. During premarital counseling, one of the first things we attempt to explore is the basis for attraction. We usually ask the couple: "How were you attracted to each other?" or "What draws you to him or her?" We rarely hear women give answers that primarily emphasize physical traits. When asked about her attraction to Robert, Jennifer aptly replied: "What is most important to me is that I feel safe with him . . . I feel confident because I know he will take care of me."

THE ONE DANGEROUS ATTITUDE: PROJECTION

Many men falsely assume that women are only interested and attracted by the same things they are. They get preoccupied with their physical appearances, getting pumped up or waxing their cars to show off in style and thus completely ignore the need to convey relational and emotional security. A related issue is the tendency to confuse physical affection with closeness. If you transfer your focus off the physical and put the same amount of energy into working on being more sensitive, open, and emotionally expressive, you will be much more appealing and attractive to a woman. It's not that women are completely disinterested in physical appearance and the initial presentation. The issue is really one of emphasis and degree.

WARNING: The Surgeon General has determined that chemistry and sexual attraction alone are not enough to create a soul-mate relationship.

2. PERSONALITY STYLE

To date, there are at least fifty-three different definitions of personality, all depending upon one's theoretical orientation. For the sake of simplicity, we want to provide a working definition of personality as follows: a pattern of behavior that represents an individual's inherent style of relating to others and to his or her environment. It includes those aspects about a person that are unique—the things that set him or her apart from others. There are many things about personality that we do not understand in terms of its origins and influences. What we do know is that it seems to be rather stable over time. The wisdom literature in Proverbs 22:6 advises parents, "Train a child in the way he should go," or more literally, "Raise your child according to his or her natural bent."

Our belief is that personality is a "natural" disposition that can be shaped in early life by family and environment. Subsequently, there are two things we want you to understand. First, personality doesn't change for adults. Oh, sure, you can tweak it a little, accentuate the positive and minimize the negative, but overall, the basic tendencies will not change. Second, compatibility in this area is not about "sameness." It is not necessary or even healthy to find someone with the same personality traits. The issue has to do with your ability to accept and adapt to your partner's personality style, assuming it will not change. Does it fit with who you are and what you value most? Can you be in agreement in light of your differences? As you evaluate this aspect, you need to come to terms with your partner's personality traits and be able to say, "Yes, this fits with my style. I can accept or appreciate this about him or her." Optimally, your personalities should bring out the best in each other the majority of the time, resulting in both being better together. If you continually find yourself operating at your worst—compromising, or displaying your worst qualities—then you need to reevaluate your compatibility.

Through our research and preparation we were struck by one consistent finding: the importance of *companionship.* One extensive survey (two thousand people) asked married couples to rank their needs in order of importance. Out of a list of more than twelve relationship needs, the second most important need for both men and women was simply *recreational companionship.* In other words, the ability to just "hang out" together was valued over such needs as communication, respect, openness, affection, and romance!

In another poll (*Time*/CNN, August 9, 2000) five hundred

single adults were asked, "What would you miss most about not being married?" Again, the vast majority (80 percent of the men and 75 percent of the women) listed *companionship* as the number one thing they would miss the most. The point is overwhelmingly clear; companionship is consistently valued above most other

> In order to have companionship, there must be a high level of compatibility in personalities.

relationship needs. In order to have companionship, there must be a high level of compatibility in personalities. Again, not identical, but compatible. We would argue that it takes more than just a warm body to hang out with or the ability to simply tolerate someone's personality style to make for a solid friendship.

Nick was enraptured by Brenda's looks—he had never been drawn to anyone quite like this one. He was also deeply impressed with her sincere passion and commitment to God. However, the more he got to know Brenda, he realized that she was quite introverted. She seemed to keep all her thoughts, feelings, and opinions to herself, to the extent that he was always playing a guessing game with her. She was withdrawn in social settings as well as in one-on-one time with him. He never knew what she was really thinking, and over time he became more and more frustrated with her. He faced a dilemma—mesmerized by Brenda on the one hand, but concerned about a personality mismatch on the other. He understood this as a make-or-break issue and therefore, rather than trying to change her personality, he had to let her go.

Let me say it in a different way: Nick was very attracted to Brenda and he felt she had solid moral and spiritual character, but he was not willing to risk spending the rest of his life with her, especially given his own tendency to be impatient and dominant. He had the foresight to consider that life is lived out in the mundane, day-to-day experiences, not in the throes of physical attraction. What do we mean by that? We mean that the majority of living takes place 24/7/365 in the everyday valley of details, not on the mountaintops of romance.

HOW CAN YOU ASSESS PERSONALITY?

Here are several ways you can assess the personality of someone you date; but keep in mind this list is certainly not exhaustive. Second, we aren't suggesting you attempt to be ultra-analytical about this process. Our emphasis is on general personality styles and traits, not inner psychological dynamics! We want to help you gather information, be aware of tools, and even encourage you to seek out professional help, if necessary, in order to guide you in your evaluation.

SELF TEST (PERSONALITY QUIZ)

We have included a series of traits so that you can rate yourself and your partner on the scale from 1 to 7. This merely represents one way to measure your own perspectives. There is no objective standard here; no right or wrong. It is purely a subjective method for you to identify your perceptions about each other. Mark an *X* to indicate your position on each continuum of opposite traits and an *O* to represent where your partner's position would be. There are two tests: one for you to complete and one for your partner. This allows each of you to have your own test and it provides a way to compare your views of each other.

THE SELF TEST (#1)

BEHAVIORAL (RELATING TO THE ENVIRONMENT)

Responsible	1	2	3	4	5	6	7	Irresponsible
Cautious	1	2	3	4	5	6	7	Impulsive
Self-assertive	1	2	3	4	5	6	7	Passive
Respects others' rights	1	2	3	4	5	6	7	Indifferent to others' rights
Organized	1	2	3	4	5	6	7	Unstructured
Realistic	1	2	3	4	5	6	7	Unrealistic
Safe	1	2	3	4	5	6	7	Reckless
Steadfast	1	2	3	4	5	6	7	Persuadable
Hardworking	1	2	3	4	5	6	7	Lazy
Selfless	1	2	3	4	5	6	7	Self-indulgent
Ordinary/Conventional	1	2	3	4	5	6	7	Eccentric
Optimistic	1	2	3	4	5	6	7	Pessimistic
In the present	1	2	3	4	5	6	7	Spacey/Out of it
Conscientious	1	2	3	4	5	6	7	Oblivious

INTERPERSONAL (RELATING TO OTHERS)

Social	1	2	3	4	5	6	7	Withdrawn
Forgiving	1	2	3	4	5	6	7	Unforgiving
Life of party	1	2	3	4	5	6	7	Wallflower/Blends in to background
Trusting	1	2	3	4	5	6	7	Suspicious
Compliant	1	2	3	4	5	6	7	Headstrong
Faithful/Loyal	1	2	3	4	5	6	7	Flighty
Pursues conflict	1	2	3	4	5	6	7	Avoids conflict
Compassionate	1	2	3	4	5	6	7	Merciless
Dependable	1	2	3	4	5	6	7	Unreliable

PERSONAL (VIEW OF SELF)

Self-aware	1	2	3	4	5	6	7	Lacks self-awareness
Humble	1	2	3	4	5	6	7	Proud
Efficient	1	2	3	4	5	6	7	Ineffective
Strong	1	2	3	4	5	6	7	Fragile
Adequate	1	2	3	4	5	6	7	Inadequate
Self-confident	1	2	3	4	5	6	7	Insecure
Independent	1	2	3	4	5	6	7	Excessively needy
Fulfilled	1	2	3	4	5	6	7	Empty
Self-assertive	1	2	3	4	5	6	7	Passive
Free to be me	1	2	3	4	5	6	7	Stifled by social expectations
Calm/Relaxed	1	2	3	4	5	6	7	Nervous

THE SELF TEST (#2)

Behavioral (RELATING TO THE ENVIRONMENT)

Responsible	1	2	3	4	5	6	7	Irresponsible
Cautious	1	2	3	4	5	6	7	Impulsive
Self-assertive	1	2	3	4	5	6	7	Passive
Respects others' rights	1	2	3	4	5	6	7	Indifferent to others' rights
Organized	1	2	3	4	5	6	7	Unstructured
Realistic	1	2	3	4	5	6	7	Unrealistic
Safe	1	2	3	4	5	6	7	Reckless
Steadfast	1	2	3	4	5	6	7	Persuadable
Hardworking	1	2	3	4	5	6	7	Lazy
Selfless	1	2	3	4	5	6	7	Self-indulgent
Ordinary/Conventional	1	2	3	4	5	6	7	Eccentric
Optimistic	1	2	3	4	5	6	7	Pessimistic
In the present	1	2	3	4	5	6	7	Spacey/Out of it
Conscientious	1	2	3	4	5	6	7	Oblivious

Interpersonal (RELATING TO OTHERS)

Social	1	2	3	4	5	6	7	Withdrawn
Forgiving	1	2	3	4	5	6	7	Unforgiving
Life of party	1	2	3	4	5	6	7	Wallflower/Blends in to background
Trusting	1	2	3	4	5	6	7	Suspicious
Compliant	1	2	3	4	5	6	7	Headstrong
Faithful/Loyal	1	2	3	4	5	6	7	Flighty
Pursues conflict	1	2	3	4	5	6	7	Avoids conflict
Compassionate	1	2	3	4	5	6	7	Merciless
Dependable	1	2	3	4	5	6	7	Unreliable

Personal (VIEW OF SELF)

Self-aware	1	2	3	4	5	6	7	Lacks self-awareness
Humble	1	2	3	4	5	6	7	Proud
Efficient	1	2	3	4	5	6	7	Ineffective
Strong	1	2	3	4	5	6	7	Fragile
Adequate	1	2	3	4	5	6	7	Inadequate
Self-confident	1	2	3	4	5	6	7	Insecure
Independent	1	2	3	4	5	6	7	Excessively needy
Fulfilled	1	2	3	4	5	6	7	Empty
Self-assertive	1	2	3	4	5	6	7	Passive
Free to be me	1	2	3	4	5	6	7	Stifled by social expectations
Calm/Relaxed	1	2	3	4	5	6	7	Nervous

SCORING THE SELF TEST

Once you complete your Self Test, take a look at your scores. Obviously, any score of 5, 6, or 7 on the scale could represent an increasing level of concern. For example, let's say your partner was a 6 on the Self-confident/Insecure scale and a 7 on the Trusting/Suspicious scale. You may have a partner who lacks self-confidence and is also highly suspicious. What are the implications? Is there a problem with trust? Why? How does it affect your relationship now or how do you think it could affect your relationship later? What needs to be done about this?

Second, look closely for any patterns or clusters of traits that seem to go together (such as Passive, Avoids conflict, and Fragile). What does this tell you about the person's ability to resolve conflict? Is this a make-or-break issue? What steps would you take to address this?

Third, compare your answers with those of your partner. See where there is disagreement and then discuss your difference of perceptions. To illustrate, assume your partner rates you as "unforgiving" and this takes you by surprise. Whether this is accurate or not is irrelevant because your partner thinks it is a problem. So, you must try to understand the basis for his or her perceptions and work with it accordingly. (Hint: this is a great opportunity to open doors of discussion between you and your partner with a spirit of workability.) Try to avoid being defensive and just allow yourselves to listen to each other regarding your perspectives. Treat this as a learning opportunity and not an exercise to beat up on each other in the midst of conflict.

OTHER METHODS FOR ASSESSMENT

If you are looking for more formal ways to assess and understand your personality styles, we would suggest you seek out a professional counselor, clergy, or psychologist who can provide other methods of assessment. Some examples include the following:

- Personality Profile (created by Fred Littauer)—This inventory offers a list of 160 characteristics that you would identify and ultimately breaks each down into four categories: Sanguine (or Popular), Choleric (or Powerful), Melancholy (or Perfect), and Phlegmatic (or Peaceful), or a combination of these four personality styles. This is a very useful, practical tool that should be taken with the aid of professional counseling.

- Taylor-Johnson Temperament Analysis—This 180-question inventory requires you to rate yourself and/or your partner on a scale to determine how closely you identify with a series of traits. For example, it will show you where you stand on a continuum between Nervous and Composed; Active/Social and Quiet; Expressive and Lighthearted; Dominant and Submissive; Self-disciplined and Impulsive; and so on. This inventory must be conducted by a professional counselor.

- Prepare/Enrich Compatibility Test—This tool is an absolute must for those thinking about engagement and particularly for those already engaged. It must be administered by qualified counselors or clergy. This inventory provides a very systematic and objective assessment of personal and relationship issues for couples. Additionally, it will give an overall snapshot of a couple's relationship strengths and areas for improvement (weaknesses).

- The Minnesota Multiphasic Personality Inventory (MMPI)—This is one of the most widely used diagnostic tools for psychological assessment. I often refer to this as the best way to get an X-ray of your psychological, mental, and emotional well-being. This 567 true-false questionnaire must be taken under the direction of a professional counselor and/or psychologist.

These assessments will either confirm what you already expected or help clarify what you couldn't quite put your finger on. They give you some objectivity and help put a label on some of the behavior and patterns you have been seeing. Once you assess yourself and your partner, then you can make decisions about your ability to accept his or her personality style. For example, let's say that you and your partner agreed to take a more formal inventory and you discovered your partner has a *Melancholic* personality style (while you are the opposite, a *Sanguine*). Although there are many strengths of the *Melancholic,* including such qualities as being deep, thoughtful, and artistic, you also know that the weaknesses of this personality style include such attributes as being moody, idealistic, unforgiving, and socially withdrawn. It would be important for you both to discuss these tendencies and make sense out of how you would adapt and accept these into the relationship. Sound like hard work? Yes, but well worth it in the long run.

For those who think this may be a little too hard or idealistic, we want you to take a long, hard look at your assumption. Too many turn a blind eye to this most important area based upon an assumption that it's just "too confusing" or "too messy." We empathize with you that this is a tough area, yet there is no excuse to enter a marriage oblivious to your partner's personality style. We don't think it is unrealistic to identify and address your partner's style and to consider whether your personalities mesh together. If you have to, take responsibility for yourselves and seek out professional help. In the end, you must be able to enter a marriage accepting your partner as is, with the assumption that personality will not change. Remember, your prayers won't change her personality. Your marriage won't change his natural disposition. Even love cannot change her personality. As a last resort, you can try to slip a rabbit's foot under his pillow at night, but if that doesn't have some kind of lasting impact, nothing will!

3. LIFESTYLE (INTERESTS AND HOBBIES)

Everyone at the party gasped when Pat and Chris walked into the room hand in hand. *This is so unnatural; they weren't meant to be together,* thought one of the onlookers. "Do my eyes deceive me?" another whispered to his equally stunned girlfriend. She replied, "No, your eyes are fine, but this is outrageous!" For the duration of the party, people continued to buzz about Pat and Chris and their first appearance on the scene.

Maybe you're not sure what's going on here and why everyone at the party was so upset. You see, Pat is twenty-five years older than his bubbly new girlfriend, Christine. Pat and Christine were oblivious to what seemed so obvious to the rest of the room—their blatant incompatibility. Now, age doesn't necessarily imply incompatibility but imagine the potential for relational mismatch. For starters, you have radical differences in recreational pursuits and cultural connecting points. Pat is more interested in Neil Diamond and playing golf, while Christine is still thinking about Britney Spears, Rollerblading, and watching MTV. Second, priorities and phase-of-life issues come in to play. Pat is preoccupied with nursing homes (for his parents) and grandchildren, while Christine is focused on nursing school and having children. Get it?

Granted, no relationship should stand or fall based upon this one component of relational compatibility. Nevertheless, this is an important consideration. An individual's lifestyle, interests, and passions (or lack of passions) will tell you three things about him or her.

EMOTIONAL HEALTH

First, lifestyle provides a clue about emotional health and personal sense of well-being. It gives you valuable information about whether someone has a balanced, zestful, passionate life. Among many of the things that account for having a healthy identity is whether or not a person is truly engaged in life.

To illustrate, think about the difference between Erica and John. Erica is active in her community, involved in church, enjoys bicycling on the weekends, loves sailing, is passionate about travel, and plans to journey to the Greek Isles this summer. In contrast, consider John, whose interests include playing video games late at night and watching movies on the weekends. He especially enjoys horror films! Get the picture?

INNER SELF

Second, lifestyle and interests will reveal a part of the inner self. Interests provide a window into the soul. In your search for a soul mate, this is going to be important information in answering the questions: What drives them? Do they live to work or work to live? What do they value most? How they spend their free time tells a lot about people. Are they creative and artistic? Do they have an appreciation for music or cars? How do they cope under stress?

PRIORITIES

Finally, interests will tell you about their priorities. Are they cultured or are they the outdoorsy type? Do they enjoy travel? What forms of entertainment are they most likely to engage in? You are trying to assess how you will be spending your "free" time together. This is where *recreational companionship* comes into the picture. Are you willing to put money, time, and energy into certain interests? It's a fair question!

ARE WE COMPATIBLE?

For those of you who like to get to the bottom line regarding relational compatibility, feel free to take the Instant Compatibility Test (ICT). Your answers are either yes or no. There should be no in between. You must score a "yes" on all five questions to be compatible; any "no" response or even some hesitation could be cause for concern.

1. Is there chemistry? To put it bluntly, are you sexually attracted to your partner? If you cannot honestly identify some inner spark or chemical attraction, then you *must* reconsider.

2. Is your relationship natural? There should be a natural fit. Conversely, if you are always having to force the relationship to work or you find yourselves dealing with "issues" and conflict more often than you have times of peace and harmony, then maybe it isn't meant to be.

3. Would this be a good friend? If you removed the sexual or physical attraction, would you be naturally drawn to this person anyway? Would you enjoy his or her company?

4. Can you accept his or her personality as is? Could you spend the rest of your life with this partner even if he or she never changed? If you find yourself wanting to change his or her personality, this could be a dead giveaway for incompatibility.

5. Would you want your kids to be like him or her? Can you envision in the future having children that turn out just like your partner? If not, then why in the world would you even think about dating or marrying this person?

 THE ONE STEP YOU MUST TAKE

Now that you have read about the Relational Compatibility Zone, you can begin to construct your love target. Look at the Relational Zone diagram and begin to identify your ideal soul mate. For example, are there personality traits that are nonnegotiable for you? Is there a personality style you must stay away from? What things tend to attract you to the opposite sex? Are you limiting yourself in this regard? What lifestyle issues should you be looking for in a partner? Which ones are negotiable? Which are nonnegotiable? Use the target and the additional lines below as you begin focusing on what is important to you in your search for The One.

THE
RELATIONAL TARGET

_____
_____
_____
_____
_____
_____
_____
_____
_____

Chapter Seven

~

Your Character Zone

"It's just sex; it's just sex." That stupid little phrase was the mantra of *Politically Incorrect*'s host, Bill Maher, during the President Clinton/Monica Lewinski sex scandal. Whenever a guest on the show would try to attach some morality or character issue to the sexcapade, Maher would respond with his "it's just sex" reductionist view of the situation. He went on to say that what a man does with his sex life and what he does with his brain are two different things entirely. In other words, enlightened Americans should be able to separate what the President does with his sex organ and what he does with his brain, and judge him on the latter, not the former.

With this kind of twisted logic, you should also judge Lee Harvey Oswald on the basis of his job performance at the Texas Book Depository and not what his trigger finger did on November 22, 1963, to assassinate President Kennedy. We need to separate what one does with the trigger finger and what one does with the mind. Try this logic the next time you get pulled over. "Oh, I'm sorry, officer. It wasn't me who was speeding, but my pesky lead foot."

The moral of the story is this: what you do matters. What you do is what you believe. You may have regrets *later*, you may wise up later, you may change your mind later, but at any given moment you always do as you believe at that moment. You can't blame lapses in character on a wayward sex organ, an itchy trigger finger, or a habitual lead foot. We see too many people in the dating scene apply this twisted logic in their quest for The One. If someone says he is a Christian or a man of integrity, some women buy it without further investigation. If you want to see what someone is really like, then observe him or her over a long period of time and in a variety of situations. How he responds over this extended period of time and how he reacts to the highs and lows of life and love will help you determine whether or not he has character. You may not need character to be elected to public office, but you do need character if you want to build a lasting relationship. This chapter will help you understand what character is, why it is so important, and how to identify it in another person.

WHAT IS CHARACTER?

Honest. Faithful. Moral. Disciplined. Responsible. These are just a few words that represent good, solid character. A wise sage once defined character as who you are when no one is looking. Character is who you are on the inside, and it's precisely good character (yours and your partner's) that will determine whether or not you will have a relationship that lasts. The greatest message ever delivered on character can be found in the Bible. Jesus set the character bar high for the entire world to see in His famous "Sermon on the Mount" talk in Matthew, chapters 5–7. Men and women from around the world, such as Gandhi, Tolstoy, Martin Luther King Jr., and Mother Teresa have sought to tackle the numerous character challenges Jesus unpacks in this watershed speech.

Jesus says you must not let lust have its way. You must have a pure heart. Jesus says you must stay committed to your mate for life. Jesus says you must be honest and practice plain speech. Jesus says you must persevere and go the second mile. Jesus says you must love your enemies. Jesus says you must give to the poor and needy, behind the scenes, not in front of others who will applaud your "generosity." Jesus says you should forgive others. Jesus says you should not be consumed by stress, but put God's agenda first in your life.

He concludes this message with a story about building a house. He says that everyone who puts His words into practice is wise because the storms of life will beat against your house with great force. People who do what Christ says will have a house that weathers storms because they have a strong foundation. Their houses have been built on a rock. But the person who ignores the character challenge of Christ is like someone who builds his house on sand. When the rain pours and the wind blows with incredible force, his house will be destroyed because it had no foundation. Character is the foundation of someone's life. If a person has strong character, she is a rock. But if she has weak character, she is unstable and shifting like the sand.

One day you will build a house with another person. No, not a physical house, but a relational house. The success of your relational house will be determined by the strength of your foundation and your partner's foundation. You may be enraptured by looks, money, and even spirituality, but if your special person does not possess rock-solid character, then your house will come crashing down when hurricane-force winds hit your life. It's not enough to have great chemistry, a wonderful friendship, and even a common spiritual life; you must also have good character to complete the package.

TAKE THE CHARACTER CHALLENGE

Several challenges in the dating process confront you. First, you need to develop your own good character. The hope is that your parents, teachers, friends, and church began the process of developing good character in you years ago. If not, and you're a recent convert to the necessity of good character, you need to work hard. There are a variety of ways, but one way to develop character is by immersing yourself in a spiritual community. In other words, commit to a local church body (commit to the church; don't shop and hop every church in town). Another way is to get involved in a Bible study, Sunday school, or perhaps a small group. Your Christian brothers and sisters and you will work together to model Christian character and to hold yourselves accountable. Character is both caught and taught, and the experience of living among an awesome group of believers will help you catch and learn the ins and outs of character.

Your next challenge in the dating process is to discern whether or not the person you are dating *owns* character. Why do we put it this way—the challenge of seeing whether someone owns good character? Because it's extremely difficult to detect whether or not someone has good character in a romantic relationship. Romance creates wonderful, magical distortions, but they are distortions all the same. We feel so enthusiastic about being in love and soaking in all those good vibrations that we forget that all of this feel-good

> It's not enough to have great chemistry, a wonderful friendship, and even a common spiritual life; you must also have good character to complete the package.

stuff will one day subside. And when it all subsides, what you are left with is someone's insides—character. Character is not something you can spot on the first, second, or that oh-so-crucial third date. You must take a long time and carefully observe this person in a variety of contexts to determine whether he or she has the stuff or not. We have come up with a series of seven questions that will help you determine your partner's CQ (Character Quotient). Don't forget, this is much more important than having a high IQ or being GQ.

THE CHARACTER TARGET

1. DO YOU RESPECT THIS PERSON?
2. HOW DOES THIS PERSON HANDLE MONEY?
3. DOES THIS PERSON HAVE ENDURANCE?
4. DOES THIS PERSON TELL THE TRUTH?
5. IS THIS PERSON RESPONSIBLE?
6. DO YOU LIKE THIS PERSON'S FRIENDS?
7. HOW DOES THIS PERSON RELATE TO
   HIS OR HER FAMILY?

DETERMINING CHARACTER QUOTIENT

1. DO YOU RESPECT THIS PERSON?

The foundation of any healthy relationship is respect and admiration. Think about people in your life that you truly admire. Perhaps it is your father or mother, a coach, a teacher, a youth worker, or your pastor. Why do you respect this person? What is it about him or her that inspires your admiration and imitation? Now, focus on the person you are dating. What are the nonphysical attributes that make this person special to you? Do you have a deep admiration and respect for them? Some people are worthy of respect and others are not.

2. HOW DOES THIS PERSON HANDLE MONEY?

It is often heard that most couples divorce for one of two reasons—sex or money. One of the most difficult areas in which to maintain harmony is the area of financial management. Usually, one partner is a saver and the other partner is a spender. When you mix that dynamic in a marital relationship, you are bound to have big problems. People have strange relationships with money. Most folks have an emotional relationship with the mean green and don't even realize it. Money is more than simply a medium of exchange. It represents security, status, and power. It is vital that you find a person who manages money well, has a budget and a savings plan. If you don't like the way this person handles money or you can't come to an agreement on how you will bridge the gap on your financial differences, then you better move on to the next candidate.

Writer Jill Gianola says, "Talking about money will help you uncover potential hot spots and develop understanding and respect for how you each think about finances." She recommends that you ask a prospective partner the following questions:

- *What does your balance sheet look like?* A balance sheet or net worth statement is simply a snapshot of your financial condition that shows what you would have left if you sold all your assets and paid off all your debts. A negative net worth is a warning sign, but be sure to investigate if debt is from school loans or a credit card bill. There is a difference.

- *What is your credit rating?* You can order a copy of your credit report from Experian and exchange yours with your partner. Someone's credit report will give you a good idea of how your potential partner manages debt and whether you will receive a less than favorable interest rate if you ever buy a house. There are many couples who would have never married (and divorced) if they would have taken this one simple step.

- *Do you want children?* Children cost around $200,000 each plus college expenses, so having kids is a financial

choice as well. This question will also lead into other
related topics: Will we both work? What's your take on
childcare? When do you want to start trying?

- *How was money handled while you were growing up?*
Many financial planners will ask this question as a way to
gauge a person's attitude toward money. Was money a
hush-hush subject in his household? Were money and
gifts used to display love and affection as a child? This
question will give you insight into your partner's
background and help you understand his attitudes today.

- *What are your financial goals?* Before you say "I do," get
a picture of what he desires for the future. How does he
feel about buying a house, saving for vacations and cars,
and developing a budget?

3. DOES THIS PERSON HAVE ENDURANCE?

One of the most difficult tasks of my job is hiring new staff
members. I (Ben) have discovered over the many years of trial
and error that it is not an exact science. In a job interview (and
that's partly what dating is—one long interview), you are trying
to assess whether or not this person has the stuff to be a great
employee and blend with the chemistry of the current team. To
make this assessment, one of the things you must do is look into
this person's past to help you determine the future. You check
out the resume and ask questions about education and work
experience. One of the things that is sometimes hard to detect is
the wimp factor. Some people are basically wimps, and when
things get tough, they will whine, cave in, or walk out. In other

words, what I'm looking for is someone with staying power. Someone who will not quit. Someone who has the character quality known as endurance.

> If you are going to spend the rest of your life with this person, you better be sure this person has the ability to make a commitment and stick by that commitment no matter what.

If you are going to spend the rest of your life with this person for richer or for poorer, for better or for worse, in sickness and in health, till death do you part, you better be sure this person has the ability to make a commitment and stick by that commitment no matter what. Too many people who are separated from their spouses on the verge of divorce come into my office complaining about how they don't feel *in love* anymore or how their needs aren't getting met. After they emote for about thirty minutes, I look them straight in the eye and say that the words *emotion* and *feelings* were not mentioned in your sacred wedding vows. Marriage is not about feeling good all the time and having your needs met all the time. Marriage is about endurance; it is about hanging in there and doing whatever it takes to make your marriage work. The ability to commit to something and never give up, come what may, is the essence of endurance.

What you have to do in the dating process is determine whether or not those you date have this invaluable character quality of endurance. Start by looking at past relationships. Do they have a best friend known for over ten years? If they have not been able to forge a lasting, meaningful relationship with someone of the same gender, the chances of them building a lasting relationship with a member of the opposite sex could be slim. Ask about educational career. Did they finish high school or college? And if they quit, what were the reasons? Look at career. Have they displayed the ability to hold down a job? Are they constantly hopping from job to job or constantly changing careers? These are a few questions to get the ball rolling and be helpful to you as you attempt to discern the endurance factor.

4. DOES THIS PERSON TELL THE TRUTH?

A recent survey revealed that the number one thing people could tolerate the least in another person was dishonesty. We are living in a day and age when lying has become a national pastime. With some, you don't know where the truth ends and the lies start. And if you are ever caught in a lie, the practice seems to be to never admit you are lying, but blame it on someone else or personally attack the one who is accusing you of the lie.

I was sitting next to an attorney at a recent baseball game. He told me that his coworkers encouraged him that if he lied, he could make more money. I could tell that he was considering the idea, so I went along with it. I said, "Hmm, that makes a lot of sense. If you lie more, you could make more money and you could pay less on your income tax and you could cheat on your wife and you could set up a phony company and scam people. Your friends are right—you really could make a whole lot more cash if you just lied a little more."

Does the person you are with tell the truth or is he or she more like this attorney? You will be able to tolerate a lot of junk in a relationship, but lying is a deal-breaker. Why is truth telling such a big deal? Because everything rides on the ability of people to tell the truth about who they are, what they do, where they have been, and where they are going. If the person you are with is not honest, how can you ever trust a word he says? If she continually lies to your face, how in the world can you trust her?

Marriage is a sacred trust between two people who are fully committed to loving each other "till death do we part," and that full commitment includes being honest with each other. Nothing erodes the foundation of a relationship more than a lying mouth. God lists it as one of the seven deadly sins.

Edward came to see me because he had caught his girl-friend, Iris, in a series of lies. He was frustrated and put out with her because this was becoming a pattern in their relationship of more than a year. Now he doesn't know if he can close the deal because of this glaring character glitch. Many times he wonders if she is seeing someone else because she is always trying to cover her tracks.

Look for someone who is transparent and seeks to tell the truth. Face it, we have all lied at some point and we all continue to do so on some level (I'd be lying if I said otherwise). But there is a big difference between a habitual liar and someone who is willing to admit lying and ask forgiveness when he fails to be completely honest.

5. IS THIS PERSON RESPONSIBLE?

Sandra Bullock played an addict in the film *28 Days*. She was sentenced to spend, you guessed it, twenty-eight days in a rehab center for getting so wasted that she drove a car through a house. During one of the group sessions, a fellow struggler asked the head counselor, "How long should you wait after rehab to begin a dating relationship?" The therapist responded with a classic answer. He said the first thing you should do when you get out of rehab is to buy a plant and take care of it for one year. Then, he said, if the plant is still alive after a year, you should go out and buy a dog. Take care of the plant and the dog for another year, and if they are both still alive after that, you can think about getting into a relationship with another person. What sound advice.

If people are not able to take care of their own lives, then there is no way they will ever be responsible enough to take care of you—or the relationship. That's why we highly recommend you don't get married straight out of high school or college. You are still developing into adulthood during this time. Get a job. Cut the strings from Mommy and Daddy. Start paying your own rent and food bills. We believe a lot of people could benefit from the plant and dog test mentioned. Getting married is a huge responsibility. You have to be responsible enough to play the role of spouse, parent, friend, lover, financial planner, psychologist, accountant, domestic engineer, and travel agent. Don't even think about making a life commitment to another person who is irresponsible. If you are dating someone right now and you feel that he or she is a slacker or someone who does not provide you with an overall sense of security, then get out now.

6. DO YOU LIKE THIS PERSON'S FRIENDS?

Maybe you are thinking, *What does that matter? I'm dating him, not his friends.* Wrong. A person's friendships are a mirror reflection of his or her character. Like-minded people hang out together—that is why they are friends, because they share something in common. If you want to get a picture of what your partner is really like, then take a long, hard look at his or her closest friends. If you do not like what you see, then just wait around a bit and those undesirable traits will manifest themselves in your sweetheart like fleas on a dog.

Before I (Ben) perform a wedding ceremony, I have the opportunity to spend about twenty minutes with the groom and his groomsmen. The groom is usually in a state of utter shock as he is contemplating spending the rest of his life with this woman in the expensive white dress, and the groomsmen are making him feel the pressure even more. On some occasions, though, the groomsmen are way out of line. Whether they are half drunk or make totally inappropriate remarks, there is something deep inside me that feels the bride is about to be betrayed. Often I feel the urge to bolt out of the room and run into the bride's quarters and tell her to call off the wedding. Why? Because I know that no matter how good, clean, and Christian this groom appears to be, there lurks the weak character of his groomsmen. Somewhere down the road, this bride to be will be wailing in tears because he is not what he appears to be.

7. HOW DOES THIS PERSON RELATE TO HIS OR HER FAMILY?

When you are about to make one of the biggest decisions in your entire life, you cannot ignore how your potential mate relates to his or her family. Does he have a healthy relationship with his mom? Does she have a healthy relationship with her dad? Also, take a good, long look at the same-sex parent of a potential mate. Research supports the idea that there is a strong connection between the parent's approach to life and his or her offspring's approach. People have a tendency to identify with the same-sex parent as well as imitate the behavior (whether or not they mean to). Additionally, you want to consider how love was expressed in the home. Was it expressed through words, gifts, physical affection, or acts of service? If this person does not display a loving attitude toward his or her family, then beware. How he views his mother, or how she treats her father, can be a good indicator of how he or she will treat you.

There is no doubt that a large number of people come from broken homes and were raised by only one parent. If this is the case with your beloved, then make sure he or she understands what kind of impact this had. Coming from a divorced home can radically affect one's view of marriage, or of the opposite sex in general. Family dynamics play a gigantic role in forming someone's character. However, let's be clear: just because someone came from a broken home doesn't necessarily mean he will not have strong character. Often, growing up with one parent can force someone to grow up more quickly and even develop good, solid character as a result.

TIMING IS EVERYTHING

You need to consider these seven questions as they pertain to your partner, over a long period of time. You don't need to start a methodical interrogation after the third date but you do want to begin a process of observation immediately. Remember, you can fake character for up to six months, but after that post-honeymoon phase, character becomes much more difficult to disguise. If you are really committed to identifying someone's Character Quotient, observe the person over the seasons: winter, spring, summer, and fall.

 ## THE ONE STEP YOU MUST TAKE

After reading this chapter, what have you learned about the importance of character? How does your partner measure up to the seven-question character quiz? Take a look at the Character Zone diagram and begin to write down your own list of non-negotiable character qualities. For more insight on this topic, check out our book *The Ten Commandments of Dating*, in which we discuss five essential character qualities that you need in a mate—he or she must be faithful, honest, committed, forgiving, and giving.

When you consider good, solid character, what are the qualities that stand out for you? What is the most important step you can take to address the Character Zone in your love life? Answer the questions on the next two pages to help you understand how vital character is.

THE
CHARACTER TARGET

1. DO YOU RESPECT THIS PERSON?

_____

_____

_____

2. HOW DOES THIS PERSON HANDLE MONEY?

_____

_____

_____

3. DOES THIS PERSON HAVE ENDURANCE?

_____

_____

_____

4. DOES THIS PERSON TELL THE TRUTH?

_____

_____

_____

5. IS THIS PERSON RESPONSIBLE?

_____

_____

_____

6. DO YOU LIKE THIS PERSON'S FRIENDS?

_____

_____

_____

7. HOW DOES THIS PERSON RELATE TO
HIS OR HER FAMILY?

_____

_____

_____

Chapter Eight

~

Your Spiritual Zone

I can't believe this guy is still alive and kicking, I thought as I listened to one of the most horrendous childhood stories of my professional career. Jason was, in every sense of the word, a true survivor. Having grown up in San Francisco without a father and living in motels with a mother who was a drug abuser, he was "raised" by his mother's boyfriends—all of whom drank and used drugs themselves. Sadly, that's just half the story! And yet, somehow, Jason managed to survive this ordeal and enter adulthood as a reasonably healthy individual with a good, steady job, and married with one child on the way. In fact, the only reason he came in to see me was for preventative reasons, in order to prepare for fatherhood.

Over the last fifteen years, I've had the privilege and opportunity to work "in the trenches," counseling all kinds of people: young and old, rich and poor, discussing every imaginable issue. And I have been consistently amazed at the triumph of the human spirit. Some have demonstrated great courage as survivors of some traumatic event or loss in their lives. Others have shown great patience as they have slowly pulled out of the depths of depression and despair. Still others have exhibited strength during a long battle with an addiction. Through this, I'm always intrigued by the fact that some people who may come from the most extraordinary circumstances seem to emerge as strong, healthy, and sane individuals. Yet others who come from fairly stable backgrounds and may experience the equivalent of an "emotional hangnail" often respond as though their whole worlds are falling apart. How do you account for this difference? What separates the men from the boys or the women from the girls? It all centers on the question: *What makes you tick?* In other words, what is the driving force behind someone's life? What is in his or her heart of hearts? Or what gives him or her a sense of meaning or purpose in life?

How would you respond to that question—*What makes you tick?* What about the person you desire to spend the rest of your life with, your soul mate? Do you know what makes him or her tick? Getting to know someone is like peeling back the layers of an onion. However, with people, unlike the onion, after peeling layer after layer, you finally get to the core. That core, that center, that something that makes someone tick, is what we call the Spiritual Zone. By the way, everyone has a spiritual zone—from card-carrying atheists to Bible-toting seminary students. Your belief system, your morals or values, your philosophy of life or religious preference, all of these elements work together to form your spiritual zone. It's the essence of who you are and who you desire to become.

It perplexes us to see hundreds of couples cruise through the dating and engagement stages of a relationship, naively ignoring this make-or-break component of building a strong, healthy marriage. The Spiritual Zone is the bull's-eye in the Love Target because ultimately everything flows from the heart. Jesus was the master at shooting a flaming arrow into someone's life. He could burn away the superficial and reveal what was in the deep recesses of the heart. This chapter will examine the importance of the Spiritual Zone, the three reasons why many people ignore this zone, and four things to look for to find a person who is truly in the zone.

WHY YOUR SPIRITUAL ZONE MATTERS

Obviously, this book is written from a Christian perspective. Our parents are Christians, we are Christians, and we are teaching our children the Christian faith as well. Our lives have been profoundly impacted by this particular belief system. It affects the way we view dating, marriage, divorce, money, work, sex, and recreation. Our faith spills over into every aspect of our lives and colors the way we see the world. When you internalize a particular religion and seek to apply its teachings to your life, it becomes much more than just a brand name. Your faith becomes your worldview.

What is a worldview? A worldview is a system or arrangement of concepts that help you make sense of the world. For example, a worldview contains concepts about what is the nature of humans, what is the worth or value of a human life, what are our origins, what is ethical, what is our destiny, is there a God, and if so, what is God like? These concepts about the basic questions of life, taken together, represent the way you view the world . . . your worldview.

A worldview is like a pair of sunglasses. If you have rose-tinted lenses, everything you see will be shaded with a rose color. If you have yellow-tinted lenses, everything you see will be shaded with a yellow color. So, your personal worldview serves as a lens by which you view and interpret the world around you. There are a myriad of factors that go into the creation of your worldview. Your parents, your education, your socioeconomics, your race, your religion, and your childhood experiences are just a few factors that contribute to the formation of your worldview.

What kinds of worldviews are out there in society? Some people possess an atheistic worldview, others a pantheistic worldview, a materialist worldview, or a Christian worldview. We would need to write another book to teach you how to detect the multiplicity of views out there; therefore, we have limited our scope to the Christian worldview in this discussion. (For more on worldviews read *The Universe Next Door*, by James Sire.) If you are a Christian, then this chapter will help you discover if the person you are going out with, or the person you plan to go out with in the future, truly shares your worldview. If you are not a follower of Christ, you still need to find out the core beliefs of your dating partner and be sure that they match with yours.

When dating, you are attempting to determine the worldview of your partner and discern whether or not it meshes with yours. It's important to note that we did not call this area your religious zone. Just because someone says he or she is a follower of Christ, Buddha,

> **Your spiritual zone should cover not only your religion and denomination, but the other variables that determine the way you view life as well.**

or Muhammad, doesn't necessarily mean that the person is a *true* believer of any of these religions. Most people claim a particular religious affiliation if asked on a survey, but relatively few would consider themselves devout, practicing followers of that religion. Your spiritual zone should cover not only your religion and denomination, but the other variables that determine the way you view life as well. Remember, when you find out what makes a person tick, you are on your way to tapping into his or her spiritual zone.

In a society where "image is everything," many people aren't willing to "go there" (to the Spiritual Zone) in a relationship. Instead, consciously or unconsciously, they choose to ignore this crucial area. As you might expect, denial rarely makes things better, and therefore ignoring the crucial, core zone of spirituality will guarantee strife and discord down the road.

ARE YOU IGNORING YOUR SPIRITUAL ZONE?

There are three reasons why you could be ignoring your spiritual zone:

1. Safety of the Silence

2. Swimming in the Shallows

3. Satisfied Just Having Sex

1. YOU ARE HIDING IN THE SAFETY OF THE SILENCE

After seven months of dating, Ginger was excited about her relationship with Bill. She felt compatible in many areas and she could recognize that Bill had strong character. However, she suspected in her heart that Bill didn't respect her beliefs in God. It wasn't as if he was openly antagonistic, but he was more ambivalent. Ginger could not bring herself to discuss her feelings about this with him for fear she would lose the relationship; she had waited so long and invested so much. Despite her worry, she went on to marry Bill, because after all, they were so right for each other in most areas. Today, she is stuck in a miserable marriage where she takes the children to church alone.

If you keep silent about this issue, you are only hurting yourself and your partner. Do you remember the onion illustration? When you peel back layer after layer of someone, you finally get to the heart (core), that most intimate part. When someone you love does not understand or affirm your faith, he or she is rejecting the most precious and sacred part of your life. It's the ultimate slap in the face to be in a dating relationship, much less a marriage, with an unbeliever who does not agree with your worldview. If you continue to keep silent and ignore the inevitable, you will pay a severe price. This is why even if God didn't say it was wrong to marry a non-Christian, you would come to eventually realize it. An unbeliever can never fully understand you. There may be compatibility and physical attraction, but the person cannot know who you really are. The price of living with a partner who rejects who you are, deep within your soul, is a price too high to pay for a lifetime. Rejection doesn't get more total, more personal, or more painful than that. It's one thing to have differences about style of clothing or hobbies. It's another thing altogether to be married to a partner who discovers the core of your being and then says,

"No, I don't want any part of that," or "No, I can't relate to that."

2. YOU ARE CONTENT SWIMMING IN THE SHALLOWS

When I was a little boy learning how to swim, I was terrified of launching out into the deep end of the pool. I felt insecure if my feet couldn't touch bottom, so I was content to play in the shallow end. I was unaware of the great adventures that awaited me in the deep—the joy of doing a flip off the diving board and the challenge of trying to touch the drain. In our dumbed-down, instant-gratification, sound-bite society, many couples wade in ankle-deep water when so much more awaits them. We are too busy to slow down, soak in the beauty of a sunset, or read a book on a weighty subject. Many couples who supposedly fall in love never even get around to discussing philosophy or theology with each other because they are preoccupied with making out, going to movies, and shopping.

Don't be content with the shallow end of the pool forever. Launch out into the deep and ask yourself and your partner some real questions: Who am I? Why am I here? Does God exist? Is it possible to know Him? What are the things that really matter in life? What are you willing to die for? What is God doing in your life? What are your hopes, dreams, and fears? These questions will help you get to know your partner on a deeper level. If you want to choose a soul mate, you can't continue to relate on a superficial level. You must find a way to connect at the core of your being. Furthermore, the purpose of marriage is about challenging and inspiring each other to grow and become better people (see Chapter 11). You cannot do this without true spiritual compatibility.

3. YOU ARE SATISFIED JUST HAVING SEX

Whenever a couple introduces sex into the relationship, it creates an illusion of intimacy. It gives the false impression of closeness and it serves as a substitute for other forms of intimacy (emotional, verbal, and spiritual). In fact, a sexual relationship outside of marriage always stunts emotional and spiritual growth because it is unnatural and out of context. Sex is a life-uniting act that must be coupled with a life-uniting commitment. Ideally, sex should symbolize that you are one with this person in every way—physically, spiritually, economically, and emotionally. When you disrobe and join your body with another person outside the safe and secure confines of marriage, you are engaging in an unnatural act. You are saying, "I want to be one with you physically, but I do not necessarily want to be one with you emotionally, economically, or in any other way."

Sex was created for total unification, not just the joining of bodies. The Bible says when you join your body to a member of the opposite sex, you are one with that person. It commands you not to be physically one until you can be one with that person in every sense of the word. It's a monstrosity to think that you can have sex with someone in the bedroom and leave your soul parked outside in the car. *Without allowing for soul connection (within the confines of a committed marriage) sex is merely a form of mutual exploitation between two people.* We encourage you to channel your sexual energy into strengthening your

> It's a monstrosity to think that you can have sex with someone in the bedroom and leave your soul parked outside in the car.

emotional bond. Be willing to expose yourself emotionally and seek to penetrate the soul first.

THREE THINGS TO LOOK FOR IN THE SPIRITUAL ZONE

As we have discovered in previous chapters, the Bible gives us little information on how to choose a soul mate. However, there is one verse in the New Testament that gives us a lot of freedom in the mate-selection process, with one definite boundary. First Corinthians 7:39 says, "You are free to marry whom God tells you . . ." No, it doesn't say that! Excuse us; it reads, "You are free to marry the one God has chosen for you before the foundation of the world . . ." Uh, no, it doesn't say that either. What the verse really says is, "A woman is bound to her husband as long as he lives. But if her husband dies, she is free to marry *anyone she wishes, but he must belong to the Lord*" (emphasis added). God gives us freedom to use our brains and choose a mate for life. What a God, to trust us with such a big decision. We have freedom (whomever we wish) within limits (they must be in the Lord).

You must choose a person to marry who is in the Lord. Second Corinthians 6:14 makes this point crystal clear: "Do not be yoked together with unbelievers. For what do righteousness and wickedness have in common? Or what fellowship can light have with darkness?" We believe, along with countless other Christians throughout the two-thousand-year history of the church, that if someone is truly "in Christ," he will be into the following three things. Please note, we are about to plunge into the deep end of the pool because the very nature of this topic (the Spiritual Zone) warrants a more serious level of discussion.

THE
SPIRITUAL TARGET

1. FAITH

When I meet with couples who are considering marriage, one of the first questions I ask them is, "When did Jesus Christ become a reality in your life?" Over the years, I've heard a wide variety of responses to that question:

> "Well, I've always been a Christian from the day I was born."
>
> "When I was twelve, I was confirmed in the _____ church."
>
> "My parents took me to church on Christmas and Easter."

"I can't remember a time I didn't believe in Jesus, Elvis, and
   America too."
"I don't know about Jesus, but I am a very spiritual person."

Many people have grown up in the church, have been
sprinkled, baptized, or confirmed, and yet still have not had a
genuine experience with Jesus Christ. Most of us would like to
believe that if you're sincere about your personal beliefs (your
religion of choice), then God will love you, and when you die,
you will go straight to heaven, no questions asked. That's an
optimistic way of looking at spiritual things, but it is not consistent with the Bible.

As God leans óver the balcony of heaven and gazes down at
the planet earth, He sees two different camps. Everyone is born
into the first camp—we are all natural-born sinners, law-breakers
by choice and by birth. Therefore, we are all under the wrath and
condemnation of God, which keep us from having relationship
with Him. The good news is, God has done something about our
sinful predicament that can transfer us from the condemned
group to the justified group and restore relationship with God.
Jesus Christ is the good news from God. He came to this planet,
lived a perfect life, died on a cross to pay the penalty for our sins,
and rose again on the third day. If you place your faith in Jesus
Christ, you will be forgiven. Which means you will be forgiven of
all of your sins—past, present, and future—and God will credit
to your account the perfect record of Jesus Christ.

You must be certain of two things. First, that you have had a
real experience with Jesus Christ, and second, that the person you
plan on being married to for the rest of your life has had a genuine

experience with Christ as well. When Jesus becomes a reality in your life, you realize that you are helpless and hopeless without Him. You humbly confess your wicked and dependent state and put your faith in Jesus as your only hope for salvation. You see for the first time in your life that it is only by grace through Christ that God is able to forgive you and make you right with Him.

We recently read a disturbing report that indicated 45 percent of those who claim to be Christians in America believe that "if you are good enough, you can earn a place in heaven." Religion, spirituality, or just trying to do the best you can will not cut it. It is through Christ alone and trusting in Him that you are forgiven and declared righteous in the sight of God. If people are really "in the Lord," they will understand faith in Christ alone. Jesus will be a reality in their lives, not just a swear word or a meek little teacher or guru. Right now, you could be rationalizing this issue to yourself: "He or she claims to be a Christian. He or she believes in God and must be in the Lord." If people are in the Lord, they will be into faith, but they will also be into this next aspect of Christianity.

2. FRUIT

If you got down on your hands and knees right now and started barking and wagging your rear end, would that make you a dog? What if you decided to sleep in your garage tonight; would that make you a car? There are many posers in the dating world who say, "I'm a Christian; I believe; I have faith in Jesus." And yet they rarely go to church; they sleep around, curse like a gangsta rapper, and get smashed every other weekend. Saying "I have faith; I believe in Jesus" no more makes you a Christian than saying "bowwow" makes you a dog. God says that faith without works is dead. To put it another way, if you truly have faith in Jesus Christ, then your life will be changed and you will produce fruit.

No, not apples, oranges, and bananas, but the fruit of the Spirit mentioned in Galatians 5:22–23. The fruit of the Spirit is love, joy, peace, patience, kindness, goodness, faithfulness, gentleness, and self-control. The fruit of the Spirit is contrasted with the selfish desires of the flesh, which are sexual immorality, debauchery, fits of rage, selfish ambition, envy, and drunkenness, just to name a few. Does the one you are seeking or the one you are with look more like the Spirit list or the flesh list?

Consider the fruit of the Spirit one by one.

- Love—Is he or she a loving person? Does he or she sacrificially love me? Does he or she seek to love others?

- Joy—Does this person have that exuberant spirit that lives in the life of a man or woman of faith? Does this person have a joy in his or her heart, even when times are tough? Happiness is dependent upon circumstances and "happenings." Joy, on the other hand, is stable and consistent in spite of the circumstances.

- Peace—Does this person have peace with God through Jesus Christ? Is this person anxious and worried all the time, or does he or she have a calming nature?

- Patience—Is this person able to delay gratification? Disciplined with his or her wallet and time? Patient with you or demanding?

- Kindness—Is this person truly kind? Whatever you do, pick someone who is kind. Someone who is cruel or has a mean streak will ruin your life.

- Goodness—Is this person basically good? Does he or she have strong morals and stand up for what is right?

- Faithfulness—This is the mark of a true believer. Someone who is always there, consistent, and honest. Is the one you are with faithful or flaky?

- Gentleness—Is this person sensitive to your needs and feelings or cold and macho?

- Self-Control—Does this person control his or her speech? Does this person control the sex drive, or is this person always testing your boundaries?

Does this list describe you? Can you say that *you* are The One? Does this list describe the one you are dating at this very moment? Isn't this what you are looking for in a mate for life? The proof of someone's faith is in the fruit pudding. Don't forget the curse word we learned in the first chapter! Compromise. If you lower your standards at this point and compromise, you will lose everything you are trying to gain in a strong marriage. The strength of your marriage will be determined by your ability to make a wise choice to marry someone who is qualified. A qualified future mate in the Spiritual Zone will be into faith and into fruit as well. Finally, this special someone "in the Lord" will be into family.

3. FAMILY

We are not talking about your biological family here or the importance of making your family a priority in your marriage; rather we are talking about the local church, the family of God. Shoppers love to hang out at malls, golfers love to hang out at golf courses, swimmers love the water, and someone who is "in Christ" loves to be at church. If you are in a relationship with someone who claims to be a Christian but is not an active member of a church, then beware. There is a chance this person is not a follower of Christ. Like-minded people enjoy being around others who are like-minded. It is that simple. If this guy or gal you are with has no desire to get involved in a church family, then it's time to think about getting out of the relationship. There is one major exception to this. Some people have been significantly hurt or spiritually abused by people in the church who claim to be "Christians." If this applies, then make sure your partner seeks to deal with this hurt and confusion so that he or she may safely seek out the security of a healthy church body.

What if you go to the Baptist church and he goes to the Catholic church? Or perhaps you are charismatic and she attends a Bible church? I tell every couple who is in this dilemma to make the decision to worship in one church. You may want to pick a neutral site or pick one or the other, but don't live under the illusion of attending separate churches and having peace at home. First, we could show

> What if you go to the Baptist church and he goes to the Catholic church? Or perhaps you are charismatic and she attends a Bible church?

141

you couple after couple who have driven a wedge in their marriage because one spouse has decided to do his or her own thing. Sure, Christians can agree on the essentials—the Apostles' Creed, the Ten Commandments—but let's face it, friends: If you cannot agree on which church to attend, your relationship is in danger. There has been and continues to be strife all over the world between "Christian" groups and their passionate disagreements over nonessential doctrines. You do not want to bring an unholy war into your relationship.

Second, there is a *huge* unforeseen factor in this equation—children. As a parent, you want to present a unified front on all sides, but especially on the spiritual front. Should you take little Johnny to get sprinkled, or wait until he walks the aisle and dunk him in the baptismal booth? What will your parents say if he doesn't get sprinkled as an infant? Or get immersed as a child? These issues seem trivial now, and many assume they'll work themselves out later. Wrong! They will only get worse. It's much easier to repair a ship at port than when it is already out to sea.

A church family will be vital to the success of your dating and marriage relationship. God has designed us to live in community. There is no place for Lone Ranger Christians or Lone Ranger Couples. If that is your MO, you will wither and die. We need the support, encouragement, and love of fellow Christians and other couples who are struggling to make this thing work. Most people will tell you to bolt, get a divorce when your marriage goes through a tough season. But a church family will encourage your commitment, provide a listening ear, or recommend a counselor or conference to attend. We have seen many marriages saved and restored over the years because the couple had surrounded themselves with close friends. On the other hand, we have seen marriages dashed on the rocks because instead of going to the church for help, they ran the other direction to seek out counsel that would tell them what they wanted to hear.

To land The One, you must hit the Spiritual Zone bull's-eye dead-center. "Well, he is almost a believer," or "She is close to coming to Christ." Remember the saying we learned as children: "Almost only counts in horseshoes and hand grenades." Be sure your choice of a mate for life is into faith, fruit, and family.

 ## THE ONE STEP YOU MUST TAKE

Do you know what makes you tick? Have you investigated this question with your partner? Have you identified the three essential elements of the Spiritual Zone? When you consider spiritual connection, what are the nonnegotiable aspects you must share with your future partner? Are you prepared to delve in to the core, spiritual zone of those you date? What step can you take to make this a priority in your life? List and expand on your thoughts in the space provided on the next page.

THE
SPIRITUAL TARGET

CHOOSING

The *One*

Chapter Nine

~

Are You in Love with the Wrong One?

$\mathscr{A}$ren't you amazed at the dangerous and downright idiotic things we will tolerate in another person when we make the false assumption that he or she is The One?

Whitney called my radio show to tell me how she was madly in love with Tom. Everything about their relationship was wonderful, except for one minor problem—he was married. After I gave her a compassionate verbal lashing, my next caller, Diedra, picked up where I left off and continued to chastise Whitney. I had a cow when Diedra later confessed to me that she had been living with a man for five years, and that he was currently cheating on her. Talk about the need to remove a two-by-four from your own eye before removing a splinter from another's. Yikes!

Now those are extreme situations, but most of us would confess (I know I do) that we have hung on to people in a dating relationship far too long, when we knew for months that it was not going to work out. One of the important steps in the process of choosing a soul mate is learning how to eliminate those who are not good candidates for a soul-mate relationship. If you can discern who is *not* The One, then you are well on your way to finding The One. This chapter will give you eight ways to know whether it is not The One and five tips on how to break it off, should you face this unfortunate dilemma. Since you can never underestimate the power of denial, let's first take a look at some reasons (or better yet, rationalizations) as to why you may be holding on to Mr. or Miss Wrong.

WHY ARE YOU STILL HOLDING ON TO THE WRONG ONE?

"I know I can fix this one." Too many sweet, innocent victims of love fall for this one and wind up married to an alcoholic, drug addict, or philanderer. If you feel the need to renovate the one you're with or reason that marriage will change the one you love, think again. Marry a person, not a project.

"But I love him." If you believe that love can conquer all, including huge credit card debt, a weak character, and a depressive personality, you are mistaken. True love allows others to experience the negative consequences of their choices and does not always cover for them.

"It's better than being alone." The first time a young woman in her twenties said this to me, I was sad and somewhat sympathetic. But after years of working with divorcées or those married to toxic people, I realize how common this kind of thinking can be. On some level, this line of reasoning is understandable. Yet when a relationship is damaging to your growth or sense of self, the cost is much greater than the short-term benefit.

"I've invested too much time and energy." When you have poured your heart and soul into another person, it is extremely difficult to let go. Who wants to start the process over again with someone brand new? I do empathize with this rationalization, but

know from experience that you don't want to forge ahead when you see major red flags.

"I'm scared of what the person might do if . . ." If you are anxious that he or she might do something crazy if you break up, then just think a little bit about what you are saying. This means you are going out with, or on the verge of marrying, an unstable person. The fact that you have these kinds of concerns about this individual should make you scared about your own lack of judgment.

"I'm afraid I will hurt the person." Hello, it's called a break up, not a love-off. In any relationship, someone may get hurt in the process. Ending a relationship is usually difficult, touchy, and painful for both parties. Sometimes healthy decisions and responsible action are painful.

"I need the financial security this relationship offers me." The Beatles were right; money can't buy you love. But it sure can buy you the illusion of security. If you continue to hang on for this reason, you will be headed for a passionless, empty marriage.

"God's called me to carry this cross." Do you really believe that God wants you to date or marry someone who is unhealthy for you? This hyperspiritual, self-righteous approach probably says more about the psyche of the person who embraces it than it does about the poor soul viewed as a "cross." In fact, some falsely reason that God's will is always the difficult and rocky path. Sometimes God does take us down a rough road, but let's not be presumptuous or foolish and assume He wants you to make a poor choice in the dating arena.

I know it is tempting to close your eyes, rationalize, and pray that things will change, but more than likely they will not. You know you are "hanging on" when you are always trying to justify your relationship or dreaming about the person you hope he or she will become. As you look at the Love Target, you may be thinking, *Well, this person hits in two out of the three zones.* Maybe the relational compatibility is there, but you are a Christian and he or she is Jewish. Or you are both Christians of strong character, but you are about

> I know it is tempting to close your eyes, rationalize, and pray that things will change, but more than likely they will not. You know you are "hanging on" when you are always trying to justify your relationship or dreaming about the person you hope he or she will become.

as compatible as Laura Schlessinger and Howard Stern. Whatever the mix, you are not hitting in all three zones. As an old pop song went, "two out of three ain't bad." It ain't bad, but it is not good enough to build a healthy, lifelong relationship. If you are stubborn or not convinced yet, then read on. Here are eight good reasons this is definitely not The One for you.

EIGHT GOOD REASONS THIS IS NOT THE ONE

1. You are not in sync spiritually. You probably remember the "I Love You" computer virus that infected millions of computers around the globe. The virus was packaged in an E-mail titled "I Love You." Because we all want to be loved, it is no surprise that more than one hundred million people opened this lethal E-mail without knowing the disastrous effects it would have on their PCs or on an entire network. In a similar way, so many people are so eager to fall in love or find The One that they ignore the Spiritual Zone all together, until they wake up one morning and realize how their entire relationship has been infected by this lack of spiritual compatibility. If you are not in sync spiritually, you cannot connect with this person heart to heart.

2. *You see major character flaws.* After listening to Darren go on and on about all the bizarre personal traits he was tolerating in his relationship with Bianca, I finally stopped him and said, "She must be incredibly good-looking." Darren was surprised and responded, "Why would you say that?" I went on to tell him that there was no other way anyone would put up with the major character flaws he mentioned, unless he was blinded by looks or sex. If someone is dishonest, mean, angry, emotionally unstable, or unfaithful, this is a sign. Don't wait for a voice from on high to move on.

3. *You are not romantically attracted.* If you are not attracted to the person you are dating, something is wrong. Don't try to be more spiritual than you are and forge ahead, hoping that things will change. Things will change; you will find someone else down the road whom you are attracted to and wonder why you settled for second best. I've seen many a "spiritual" man or woman hang on to a potential marriage partner for years, praying that God would zap them with the ability to be attracted to their partner. I've talked to women whose marriages ended in divorce because they were attracted to his "love for God," but turned off in every other way. If you think romantic attraction is unimportant to God, then I challenge you to read Song of Solomon.

4. *You are having to work too hard.* It is often stated that any

good relationship requires hard work and continual maintenance, but if you are constantly striving during the dating stage to have fun and to experience a sense of unity, then your marriage will be a living Alcatraz. Vince and Sandy are a perfect example of a couple who has it all: they're attracted to one another, both love God, and both have evidence of strong character. However, their relationship is out of balance. It's all work and no play. It's too serious and seems to require constant analysis of motives and intentions. The daily miscommunication and evaluation rob them of the necessary joy and laughter that any good soul-mate relationship should have.

5. *You are constantly fighting.* Julia and Paul dated each other for more than a year, but their relationship was more like a non-stop boxing match than a romance. Paul was headstrong and Julia was contentious. For some reason, they could not go out in public without getting into some kind of quarrel. In private, these quarrels escalated to all-out war and their problems were never fully resolved. If you are in a relationship that is characterized more by your quarrels than your intimate conversations, then you are headed for trouble. There needs to be healthy conflict in any relationship or you cannot grow, but if your relationship is one big battleground, that is a sign of incompatibility.

6. *You have been abused.* If you have been physically or verbally abused by your dating partner, get out, move on—no questions asked. We have zero tolerance for men who would strike, push, or verbally abuse their girlfriends (and you should too). I don't care how many times he said, "I'm sorry; it will never happen again." Don't give him a second chance. You do not want to be a feature story of domestic violence on the evening news.

7. *You are not top priority in his or her life.* Ashlyn always felt she was low on the totem pole of Terry's priorities. She was right. He never did anything special for her on Valentine's Day or her birthday. He would constantly go out with the guys on the weekends and squeeze time in with Ashlyn whenever it was convenient for him. Amazingly, she allowed this to continue, until one day she got up enough nerve to call it off. Terry was stunned and pleaded to get back together, but she was tired of being treated like leftovers. Catch a clue from Ashlyn. If you are not a priority in his or her life today, you never will be.

8. *You are constantly changing to please him or her.* A chameleon is a tiny lizard that blends into the color of its environment. If it is perched on a gray rock, then its skin will turn gray. If it is on a brown leaf, then its skin will automatically turn brown. When you are trying to change your personality, friends, hair color, or tastes in movies just to please the person you are going out with, then you are a chameleon dater. You want someone to be attracted to you for who you are, not the phony skin you are wearing to blend in and make the other person feel good. One day, your true colors will show.

The greatest temptation you will face (or perhaps the greatest temptation you are facing at this very moment) is to blow off some or all of the eight good reasons you just read. Take a look at some of the more common justifications: "It's so hard to find someone out there who has it together," or "Once we get married, he or she will start going to church, being more romantic, expressing his or her feelings . . . Once we get married he or she will stop drinking with friends, cheating on me, hitting me, criticizing me . . ."

Listen, please. Marriage will not change this person. Marriage

Marriage will not change this person. Marriage will not change your so-so relationship into an intimate partnership. Marriage will magnify your problems, not cure them. will not change your so-so relationship into an intimate partnership. Marriage will magnify your problems, not cure them. Once you are married, these *eight reasons* to break up will turn into grounds for separation or divorce. Sure, it will be painful to call it off, but it will be much more painful to get a divorce or attempt to endure an unhealthy, stagnant marriage. If you know this is not The One, but you aren't sure about how to end it, then follow these guidelines.

HOW DO YOU BREAK IT OFF?

Many people who find themselves in an unhealthy relationship attempt the avoiding or passive-aggressive approach (they simply do nothing). Instead of seeking closure, they just stop calling, start refusing to go out, and try to let the relationship die without any confrontation. Others will cop out and use the "God told me we should break up" line, thus putting the blame on God. If you know that the relationship is over in your heart and mind, then be respectful and take action. Here are some helpful guidelines on how to break up.

1. IMMEDIATELY

Do not waste any more of your time or your partner's time by prolonging the inevitable. You have to work through the fact that feelings will get hurt, not everyone is going to be happy, and life in general can be painful. If you play games and hold on, all you are doing is enlarging the emotional wound. Sure, you are a month away from your one-year anniversary or it's too close to Christmas or it's the day after Groundhog Day or your partner just got laid off. There will always be excuses as to why it's not the right time. It is never a good time to break up. But now is always better than later. That's why you must act immediately!

2. HONESTLY

Be open, honest, direct, and sincere. Get to the point and don't linger in the realm of ambiguity. Make sure you do so in the spirit of letting your yes be yes and your no be no.

3. TACTFULLY

This is not your time to get even for every cruel thing that has been done to you. Nor is it appropriate to get into the specific and gory details, or it will turn into a "let's see if we can work this thing out" session. Be honest but tactful. Do not read off a list of every reason as to why he or she is not The One. If you are emotional, take a deep breath and try to calm down. You may want to write out what you are going to say and read it to the person. Be challenged by Ephesians 4:29: "Let no unwholesome word proceed out of your mouth, but only what is edifying for the need of the moment. Remember to exhibit compassion and grace" (our paraphrase).

4. COURAGEOUSLY

You can do it. Breaking up is one of the most difficult things in the world to do. You may love this person on some level; there have been some good times shared, and he or she may be a won-derful person in many ways, but don't lose sight of the fact that you are not a match. You are doing the other person a favor as well as yourself. Do you want to spend the rest of your life with someone you know can never be your soul mate? Would you want the person you are about to break up with to spend the rest of his or her life with someone who can never be his or her soul mate? Don't forget that courage is the ability to do something despite your fear. It is not courageous to do something you are not afraid to do. Be strong and courageous. It may be one of the best decisions you ever make.

5. COMPLETELY

This is where most people balk or hesitate. To mix metaphors, they act as if they are going to punt the relationship—but wait a minute, ladies and gentlemen, I do believe it's a fake! A fake-punt breakup is when you say it's over, but you call the next week to see how he or she is doing. Or you send an E-mail or call a month from now when you are feeling lonely. Another way to fake punt is to say, "The timing is just not right, perhaps in the future . . ." Don't play games with someone's heart. If you still have some form of ongoing communication with your ex, then you are not officially broken up yet. This postrelationship/ relationship syndrome is pandemic with daters who do not want to burn their bridges. You can't be "good friends" with your ex; you have gone too far to go back to a superficial kind of friend-ship. When you call it off, be sure it is a clean break. No follow-up phone calls, E-mails, letters, or casual cups of coffee to "just see how he or she is doing."

When it's time to end it, don't delay. Do it immediately, honestly, tactfully, courageously, and completely.

 ## THE ONE STEP YOU MUST TAKE

Looking back over your relationship history, what has been your style or pattern of breaking up? If you feel convicted about your current relationship and you know it's time to break it off, what do you need to do in order to implement the guidelines mentioned? Use the space provided to take action.

_____

_____

_____

_____

_____

_____

_____

_____

_____

_____

_____

_____

Chapter Ten

~

How to Keep
The One

$\mathscr{O}$kay, so you're pretty sure you have found The One. You've considered all the major issues and you've confirmed a natural fit: you have strong relational compatibility and good character, and you connect in your spiritual zone. You have been wise, discriminating, cautious, and prayerful. Congratulations! But now what? Do you wait a little longer just in case? Do you jump in to marriage feetfirst? We want to help you take it to that ultimate place—marital success.

This chapter has a twofold purpose. First, we will offer suggestions on how to manage that delicate time from *exclusivity* through *engagement*. Second, we will offer realistic guidelines to help you enter marriage with a foundation of strength. Once you believe you have found The One, this phase of your relationship is crucial, as you are already building a foundation for your future marriage. Many assume they can start laying the foundation during the first year of marriage. What they don't understand is that the foundation has already been laid. Issues of respect, safety, trust, conflict resolution, and expectations, to name a few, are already in process. Once you are married, the cement is dry and you now begin the task of framing your house of marriage. Thus, the premarital stage is all too important and shouldn't be taken for granted. It is a time to assess the strengths and weaknesses, learn about each other, establish healthy patterns, and affirm the security of the relationship. In addition, it is finally appropriate to begin to seek God together and nurture your soul and spiritual connection.

Brad met Karen five years ago in their first business class together. They felt an immediate attraction and started seeing each other exclusively that semester. From that time, they have been together without any separation. They even moved to the same city after completing their studies. When I first met Brad, he told me he was "unofficially" engaged to Karen and expected to be married soon. That was four years ago! I recently ran in to them at a restaurant and thought, *Surely they have children by now.* I was wrong. I stood incredulous as I listened to Brad explain that he was still unsure about marriage (Karen later confided she was growing impatient and losing some confidence). As we talked at length, I discovered they had hit the bull's-eye of the Love Target early on; they had what it takes for a successful marriage and yet they were on the "perpetual engagement program." Why? The main reason he gave me suggested they were waiting for some sign from God to confirm their union.

This is an excellent example of the kind of thinking that gets people into trouble. Brad and Karen already had their sign. In fact, they had numerous "signs" and natural confirmations throughout the five-year romance. There were no red flags. This was a perfectly good relationship and yet he wouldn't take it to the next level. Brad needed to hear the following don'ts and do's of keeping The One.

THE DON'TS OF KEEPING THE ONE

1. Don't wait for a voice or sign from heaven. If you have dated exclusively for two or more years, you're out of college, and you know that you connect in the three love zones, there is no need to drag out the inevitable. In fact, you may be doing more harm than good. At some point your faith and caution begin to look like doubt and fear. You could be communicating the wrong message by playing it too safe and therefore planting seeds of insecurity. If Brad and Karen finally tie the knot, they will have to work through Brad's prolonged ambivalence and the insecurities it has produced. Most often it is the man who prolongs by offering one rationalization and excuse after another in order to buy time. This seemingly "rational" approach can actually be a cover for a lack of faith, confidence, or security.

2. Don't pressure your partner if you are within the two-year time frame. We obviously affirm the need to take your time in the dating process, but if you are highly ambivalent after two or three years of exclusive dating, you need to address the underlying issue (refer to Chapter 4). Sometimes, it is not unusual for one person to be more certain about the relationship than the other. Assuming you are somewhere within the first six and twenty-four months of the relationship, you may have a strong conviction that he or she is The One much sooner than your partner. The worst thing you can do is try to manipulate the other person's feelings or challenge his or her thinking too soon. You should give your partner the freedom to evaluate the relationship on his or her own time (within reason). Again, we could give numerous examples of perfectly good relationships that went awry all because one of the partners was too eager and too desperate to take the relationship to the altar before it was mutual. This brings up an important question about when it is okay to discuss commitment and engagement. Read on and we will address this before the end of the chapter.

> **You must be willing to play out your relationship on the stage of life in front of your friends, family, and those who care about you.**

3. *Don't isolate yourselves.* Whenever we encounter couples who isolate themselves and keep their relationship ultra-private, it usually signifies a level of immaturity or it indicates a possible warning sign. Some are tempted to ignore their friends and hide in seclusion with their beloved. After all, the thinking goes, *I've found my soul mate and he or she is all I need.* When you think you have found The One, don't exclude others from your lives together. You need to be willing to expose your partner and your relationship to your circle of friends, family, and close, trusted advisors. People who care about you will give you valuable feedback about your relationship, including your strengths as well as your growth areas. When you surround your relationship with supportive friends and family, you give them the opportunity to support and encourage you toward building a lasting marriage. You must be willing to play out your relationship on the stage of life in front of your friends, family, and those who care about you.

4. *Don't experiment with living together.* In our permissive cul-

ture, this advice may hit you where it counts. In this day and age of moral relativity, the predominant (conventional) wisdom encourages couples to test their compatibility by living together. Cohabitation continues to become the prevailing relational trend, championed by many secular relationship experts. In fact, roughly five million couples live together today compared to only 400,000 couples who lived together in the 1960s, according to the Census Bureau. To put it another way, more than half of first marriages are now preceded by cohabitation. Ironically, according to a recent study by the National Marriage Project at Rutgers University (September 1999), "living together is not marriage friendly." This study states that couples who live together before marriage are 48 percent more likely to divorce than those who don't. Among the findings was that people who cohabit report lower levels of happiness and much greater chances of domestic violence. Another study *(Annual Review of Sociology,* summer 1999) conducted by Pamela Smock, Ph.D., at the University of Michigan finds that five out of six cohabiting couples end their living arrangement within three years. In other words, the overwhelming majority of cohabiting couples simply break up! Sadly, the ones that do finally make it to the altar are up against extremely bad odds. By definition, most live-in relationships are unstable and lack commitment. In spite of the soaring trend, it is no wonder that this approach is faulty!

A BETTER WAY TO CLOSE THE DEAL

When you and your partner have a reasonable sense that you are meant to be together, besides avoiding the don'ts, we would like to offer four critical guidelines (the do's) to help you prepare for a successful lifetime union.

1. APPOINT AN ADVISORY BOARD

One of the most important things you can do to enhance your odds of success is to surround yourself with a group of people who can support you and offer priceless feedback—we call this an advisory board. You see, we were made for community, to be part of something greater than ourselves. Over the last century, we as a people have become more and more isolationistic and individualistic, which has led us to be more private about our intimate relationships. Fifty years ago, this concept of including community was natural and automatic. Back then, it seems everybody was involved in the love life of a given couple. Family members, neighbors, pastors, ministers—all had a hand in bringing people together, keeping them accountable, and encouraging their growth toward marriage. Now, it goes against your natural inclinations and you probably wince at the idea, but you need to surround yourself with people who will assist you in the process of uniting as one. Because it feels unnatural, making your relationship a part of the larger community has to be an intentional process. This is what we mean by appointing an advisory board.

We hope it is already understood that God Himself is to take the position of Chairman of the board. We assume you will be prayerful and sensitive to God's true leading as you submit to His authority and continue toward the path of engagement and ultimately marriage. To help you discern God's leading, we would suggest that you pick up a copy of Gary Friesen's book *Decision Making and the Will of God*.

Next, appoint your closest, trusted friends and family members to aid in this important decision. We would suggest that each of you seek out those people who know you best and who are not afraid to tell you the truth. Make sure you appoint those people who interact with you regularly as a couple. That way, they have a firsthand account of the relationship in context. As such, they can offer objective perspectives based upon what they observe, and not from secondhand information you have told them about the relationship.

Finally, we encourage you to include your parents or parental figures, those who have your best interests at heart. Of course, there is a balance to including them in this process. On the one hand, it is essential to get their blessing. And they can't possibly provide an honest, objective perspective unless you invite them to spend time with and get to know your partner. On the other hand, they should not make the final decision for you. If you are seeking your parents' "permission" in the strict sense of the term, then you probably aren't ready to get married. Conversely, when you seek their support and you are genuinely open to their input and observations, then you are mature, wise, and probably ready to start your own family. We respect the fact that some (perhaps many) of you do not have parents that are available. This could be due to a number of reasons, including death, geographical distance, or they are just not emotionally healthy enough to provide the perspective and support you need. In these circumstances, we suggest you seek out an older, married couple who can serve as mentors to you in this process. If you sincerely seek this out, God will provide.

TIPS FOR KEEPING FAMILY INVOLVED

Keep communication lines open. Men, especially, must work hard at communicating with parents and family. Tell them everything you can about your partner. What is so special about your beloved? What is her family history and background? Why are you drawn to her?

Visit often. Spend as much time together as possible. Plan trips together and look for opportunities for extended time away. Err on the side of overexposure.

Provide one-on-one time. Allow and plan for your partner to spend one-on-one time with each parent.

2. DEFINE THE RELATIONSHIP SOONER THAN LATER

When you have been in an ongoing relationship for a period of one year or more (assuming you are at least twenty-two years of age), it is certainly legitimate to begin the process of defining the relationship. As we have stated, this is not a time to pressure your partner for a commitment to marriage, but it is a time to be open, honest, and direct about your expectations for a future together. Obviously, the longer you've been in the dating scene and the older you are, the more proficient you become at eliminating those who

> If you have found someone with all the potential to be The One, until you have been dating for at least a year, you have no basis for real love.

are not The One. Remember, if you have found someone with all the potential to be The One, until you have been dating for at least a year, you have no basis for real love. Prior to one year, you may be infatuated, or "in lust." But make no mistake, real love takes time. Once you decide to define the relationship, you must seek to clarify your thoughts, feelings, and intentions regarding the future of the relationship.

One of the most prevalent relationship killers is the hidden expectations and unspoken assumptions in many otherwise promising relationships. Too often people will stay in a holding pattern or let the more passive partner dictate the length of the dating. Unfortunately, this is not out of respect as much as it is out of fear. Don't be afraid to gently confront your partner about lack of communication, clarity, or follow-through if this describes him or her. The luxury of having free-choice mate selection (as opposed to arrangement) is the length of time you have to get to know each other and make wise choices based upon discernment. However, some take this luxury too far and spend seven years "getting to know" their partner. This is taking a good thing too far. Eventually, this can become counterproductive and you may reach a point of no return.

3. Seek Relationship Counseling (ASAP)

Isn't it ironic that an individual must go through a rigorous process of education and training before receiving a driver's license to operate a motor vehicle, yet a couple may get legally married without any training, education, or proof of responsibility? This is Twilight Zone material. Based upon our national average of marital failure, and because of the resulting ramifications, it should be

> Once you and your partner believe each other to be The One, then it becomes critical that you seek out pre-engagement or pre-marital counseling as soon as possible.

a national law for couples to receive some form of counseling and education before their decision to marry. In fact, some states (Oklahoma and others) have already adopted this law for couples who plan to marry, and we hope the trend continues.

Once you and your partner believe each other to be The One, then it becomes critical that you seek out pre-engagement or pre-marital counseling as soon as possible. If I had a nickel for every couple that called me for "counseling" after their wedding invitations were already sent out, I'd be hobnobbing with Donald Trump off the coast of France. Quite frankly, it verges on presumption and arrogance to think that a couple can casually "waltz" in to premarital counseling five weeks before their wedding date and expect to achieve significant results. The whole point of counseling is to confirm, clarify, and objectively sort out the wisdom of this monumental decision. It is also a time to identify strengths and weaknesses of the relationship as well as identify the issues that each partner will bring to the relationship. Granted, one of the greatest concerns that couples encounter is the fear that counseling will pick apart and destroy their relationship. Keep in mind that a counselor is not the bad guy wanting to interrogate or tear you down, but is there to support you and help you. Truthfully, it is uncommon for a couple to actually break up due to counseling except in rare cases where it is apparently warranted.

There is no greater investment than the opportunity to sit down with a professional counselor or pastor and discuss this most important decision of your life. One of the things we often warn couples about is that within the first week after returning from the honeymoon, you practically have grounds for divorce! It begins with that sinking feeling that somehow you've been deceived ("You're not what I thought"), not to mention that gender differences and selfish motives start to emerge. The point is, the time to prepare for the disillusionment starts before marriage.

4. Nurture the Relationship

A committed relationship is no haven for the lazy. It's certainly not a place where you can sit around like a queen or king and be fed grapes while being fanned by a harem and never lift a finger. A relationship takes work, and it is only as good as what you are willing to invest. As much as a plant needs sun, soil, and water to live and grow, so too a relationship needs even more nurturing. Now is the time to nurture the relationship. Get actively "engaged" in the process of helping your partner grow and become a better person. Seek to develop and mature your relationship. Don't be content to ride on the coattails of infatuation and romantic love—get busy establishing and building that soul-and-spirit connection.

Once you have discovered you are spiritually compatible, you need to work on developing and growing that aspect of your relationship together. Buy books or devotionals, go to relationship conferences, and seek married mentors in order to grow relationally and spiritually together. Let us recommend a couple of good books if you are at this stage. One of the best premarital books available is *Saving Your Marriage Before It Starts* by Drs. Les and Leslie Parrott. For those who want to plunge into the theological and philosophical depths of marriage, take a look at *The Mystery of Marriage* by Mike Mason.

 ## THE ONE STEP YOU MUST TAKE

If you are in a relationship you think has the potential to be The One and have spent adequate time letting the relationship develop, evaluate your relationship against this chapter. Take an inventory of the do's and don'ts as they apply to your relationship. Which don'ts are currently a part of your situation that you may need to mend?

_____

_____

_____

_____

_____

_____

_____

_____

_____

_____

Chapter Eleven

~

Are You Ready?

While I was working on my master's of divinity in seminary, there were three pastors whom everyone looked up to as the be-all and end-all. These men had successful churches, books, and ministries that reached around the globe. They were household names in evangelical circles. Today, some fifteen years later, all three of them are divorced. Did they know the Bible? You bet; Greek and Hebrew included. Did they have a consistent devotional life? Yes. Were they good men? Absolutely. But somewhere something went wrong on the home front and they lost the most important battle of their lives.

Divorce can happen to anybody at anytime. Just because you grew up in a Christian home where your parents have been married for thirty-plus years does not mean you are immune from divorce. Just because you and your fiancé are both believers does not mean you are immune from divorce. Just because we are so-called relationship experts does not mean we are immune from divorce. The divorce rate in the church is just as bad or worse than the divorce rate in society. If you think, *This will never happen to me,* then you are to be pitied. You are not in touch with the dark side of your personality.

One of the ways you can prevent divorce is by making a wise choice for marriage. How many lives could have been spared the unnecessary trauma and pain of divorce if people would have only taken more time in the dating process to really get to know their potential partners? We cannot stress this point enough—if you want to greatly increase your odds of having a successful marriage, then choose a qualified soul mate. Choose a person who hits in all three love zones—Relational, Character, and Spiritual. Don't settle for two out of three and hope that the other zone will be actualized once you are married. Stay faithful to the process of connecting with a person in all three areas of the Love Target and you will be well on your way to building a lasting marital relationship.

The second most important principle for preventing divorce is to understand the reality of covenant marriage. Far too many couples breeze into marriage without a clear understanding of the nature of that relationship and what is required to make it work. Making a wise choice is a critical step, but it is not a stand-alone guarantee. Just because you have found a soul mate doesn't mean you can put your relationship on cruise control and expect to have a smooth ride for the rest of your life. You must buckle your seat belts tightly and prepare yourself for one of the most difficult challenges of your life.

To make this journey called marriage well worth the trip, you must get ready for the following three realities:

> **Too many couples breeze into marriage without a clear understanding of the nature of that relationship and what is required to make it work. Making a wise choice is a critical step, but it is not a stand-alone guarantee.**

1. GET READY FOR HOLINESS

Martin Luther was one of the most influential Christian leaders in the history of the church. He led the Protestant Reformation when he nailed his Ninety-five Theses on the Wittenburg door. Because of his actions he was excommunicated from the Roman Catholic Church and had to go into hiding for a period of time in order to protect his life. After all the trials and tribulations of the Reformation, Luther married a former nun late in life. Despite all the suffering and persecution he experienced during his tumultuous life, this great man said that marriage was the most refining process he had ever endured. It was not the fact that he was kicked out of the only official church of the day in which he lived; it was not even having his life threatened; it was marriage itself, learning how to love and serve his wife, which made him more mature than all the other pressures he had to embrace.

The problem is, we have bought into the silly, yet dangerous, notion that marriage will make us happy. What if, as author Gary Thomas puts it in his book *Sacred Marriage*, "God intended marriage not to make you happy, but to make you holy"? Fortunately, happiness and holiness are not mutually exclusive. Rather, it is how we view marriage before we say "I do" that will greatly affect how we will respond to the challenges once we are married. We need a radical paradigm shift to change the way we view marriage. Marriage is not primarily about feeling happy every day. Marriage is not primarily about "getting your needs met." Marriage is not primarily about "getting the love you deserve." Marriage is not primarily about "getting the sex you want." Marriage is a 24/7/365 marathon designed by God Himself to knock off your rough edges

> **Marriage is a 24/7/365 marathon designed by God Himself to knock off your rough edges and reform your selfish nature in order to make you holy.**

and reform your selfish nature in order to make you holy. Marriage is all about commitment, giving, serving, forgiving, and laying down your naturally selfish desires to live for another person. Can you imagine trying to do these things without a solid relationship with God or without true spiritual compatibility? Yes, Martin Luther was correct; marriage is the most sanctifying experience in the Christian life. There is nothing like having a full-length mirror (your spouse) following you around every day, reflecting back to you just how self-centered you really are. If you are not ready for this kind of exposure, then don't even think about getting married.

2. GET READY FOR SACRIFICE

Many well-meaning engaged couples expect marriage to be one big treasure chest, filled with all kinds of warm fuzzies and special treats. They hope that marriage will enable them to get the unconditional love they never received from their parents. Many expect the process of emotional intimacy to be a nice, warm bubble bath. Still others expect to have every sexual fantasy fulfilled on a daily basis. Some couples, once they are married, go into shock when they discover the undeniable truth that marriage is not about getting anything (at first), but giving everything. Jesus says, "No one has greater love than this, that he would lay down his life for a friend" (our paraphrase). Marriage calls you to this high level of love and sacrifice. It is not about what you will get, but what you will give.

Mike Mason, in his excellent book *The Mystery of Marriage*, writes:

> The fact of the matter is that holy matrimony, like other holy orders, was never intended as a comfort station for lazy people. On the contrary, it is a systematic program of deliberate and thoroughgoing self-sacrifice. A man's home is not his castle so much as his monastery, and if he is treated like a king there, then it is only so that he might better be enabled to become a servant. For marriage is intended to be an environment in which he will be lovingly yet persistently confronted with the plainest and ugliest evidence of his sinfulness, and thus encouraged on a daily basis to repent and to change.

Since many of us have grown up in times of relative peace and prosperity, we know very little of what it means to sacrifice. Once you are married, the shock of what it takes to live sacrificially for your mate can be overwhelming. If you are not ready to surrender your will and your rights to serve another person, then marriage is simply not for you. Marriage is a treasure chest in many ways, but it is initially empty at the beginning of a marriage. And it is what you put into this relationship, through sacrificially giving to one another, that will make your marriage shine. Paradoxically, it is only once you understand and yield to this process of giving and serving sacrificially that you are able to reap the richest rewards of the relationship treasure chest.

3. GET READY FOR COMMITMENT

If we had to pick one word to sum up a successful marriage, it would be *commitment*. Tragically, we have forgotten the meaning of this word in our culture, which has plunged us into a commitment crisis. There are commitment-phobic men and women who fear losing control of their lives and so will never take the risk of getting married. There are single men who impregnate women and run from the commitment of parenting. There are young women who abandon their children, running from the responsibility of being a mother. There are hundreds of thousands of divorced men and women who simply quit on their marriages because their own emotional needs were not being met. We have become a nation of self-centered people who are too consumed with immediate gratification, and our children are paying the price.

Commitment in marriage is simply an unconditional agreement to stay in that relationship for life. You must resolve to stay in your marriage for the rest of your life, no matter what (certainly there are some exceptions: severe abuse or repeated infidelity). Take a long, thoughtful look at the following phrases taken from wedding vows. You are making a commitment . . .

> "for better or for worse"
> "for richer or poorer"
> "in sickness and in health"
> "to love and to cherish"
> "till death do we part"

Notice what is missing. There is no mention of feelings and emotions in the vows. There is no mention of getting your needs

> There are commitment-phobic men and women who fear losing control of their lives and so will never take the risk of getting married.

met. There is no mention of not feeling in love anymore. There is no Plan B, no back door, no escape clause, no what-if. Marriage is a lifetime commitment, "till death do we part," to unconditionally love an imperfect person. Are you ready for this type of commitment?

You must understand what the marriage commitment is all about or you will give up before your relationship ever has a chance to grow and develop. The commitment you will make is not so much about your commitment to one another. Though you are committed to love one another, there will be many times you do not feel like being committed to your spouse. This commitment you will make is not so much about your commitment to God. There will be times when you don't feel like being committed to God (thankfully, He is faithful when we are faithless). This commitment is to the very nature of the relationship itself. God intended marriage to be for life. He created it as a permanent, irrevocable relationship. So, when you don't feel like being committed to your spouse or to God, it will be your commitment to the relationship itself that will see you through. Are you ready to make this lifelong commitment to your soul mate? Are you ready to love, sacrifice, and hang in there, no matter what happens?

Are you ready to take this radical step? Are you ready for the intensity of commitment, holiness, and sacrifice this decision requires? We know what you are thinking. *Oh, Ben and Sam, lighten up, would you! You don't understand. Our relationship is different. We are not going to experience the pain, problems, and pressures you guys talk about. We are so compatible and so spiritual that we will sail through marriage as though we were on God's Love Boat.* If you feel this way, please put down this book immediately and immerse your head in a bathtub full of ice and water, and hold it there until you come out of your denial. We are tickled pink that you found your soul mate, you are hitting in all three love zones, and you are making a wise choice. But do not go into your marriage with blinders on thinking it will be one long, romantic date. It will demand every ounce of strength, emotion, passion, and supernatural intervention you can muster to have a wonderful, blessed marriage.

There are few experiences in life that are as demanding on your mind, body, and soul than marriage. If you choose the right person and prepare yourself for the trinity of Holiness, Sacrifice, and Commitment, then you are well on your way to having an awesome marital relationship. Too many times we have the formula wrong and think marriage automatically equals satisfaction and happiness when in reality it is the work of sacrifice, giving, and forgiving that results in the rewards of a successful marriage. The good news is that it is through this crucible of marriage you do experience true joy and find that you have built a soul-mate relationship.

> **Too many times we have the formula wrong and think marriage automatically equals satisfaction and happiness when in reality it is the work of sacrifice, giving, and forgiving that results in the rewards of a successful marriage.**

When Cortez came to the New World, he was concerned that his men would want to retreat and go back home once they faced the dangers and hard times of this mysterious new land. This great explorer knew that people desire to return to the safe and secure when confronted with great suffering and sacrifice. So, when they landed on the sandy shores of Mexico, Cortez ordered a small crew of men to row back to the big boats and burn them. After burning all their ships, Cortez and his men knew that there was no turning back, no quitting. If you have not burned all your ships, you are not ready for this commitment called marriage. Friends, that is what it is all about—cutting off any other option in order to stay committed to the relationship regardless of the dangers and hard times you will face. Have you burned your ships? If so, you are ready for the adventure of a lifetime, and you will be surprised by the treasures you will discover along the way.

Epilogue

~

How to Guarantee You Will *Not* Find Your Soul Mate

$\mathcal{E}$ven as we sit down to write this summary, a new television show called *Temptation Island* is airing for the first time on *Fox*. (We hope the show is a distant memory by the time you read our book, but we haven't bet any money on it.) The theme of this raunchy reality TV show is to find a group of committed couples, transport them to an exotic island, and surround them for two weeks with some of the best-looking and most sensual men and women on the planet in an attempt to lure them away from their partners. Supposedly, this is the ultimate test for identifying your commitment and love for one another.

What can we say? Hogwash? Please! How absurd will it get? The saddest part is, some people will actually use some version of this ridiculous method to try to identify or confirm the true love of their lives.

So we are inspired to take one final look at the important principles for finding your soul mate. This time, we are really going to have fun with them. Let's look at the principles from the reverse angle in order to bring the truth into sharper focus. In the spirit of the outrageous *Temptation Island*, here are five faulty principles for finding the love of your life—otherwise known as the Five Ways to *Miss* Finding Your Soul Mate:

1. ASSUME THERE IS ONLY ONE TRUE SOUL MATE

This assumption will help put you in an endless and frustrating quest for that one special person. As long as you hang on to the illusion that your "missing half" exists out there somewhere, you'll be distracted and miss out on many other potential relationships. While you're at it, you might as well look for the Fountain of Youth, the Holy Grail, and even the lost city of Atlantis. When you invest your time, energy, hopes, and dreams into such futility, we promise that you will *not* find what you are looking for. You could also miss out on vital opportunities to deeply connect with others along the way. Remember as we stated in the introduction, there are many forms of relationship that can have that soul-mate quality. Of course, when it comes to marriage, there should be many potential soul mates and your goal would be to wisely choose one out of many potential candidates.

2. REFUSE TO TAKE PERSONAL RESPONSIBILITY FOR YOUR LOVE LIFE

Whatever you do, please avoid taking ownership of your life or your relationships. Expect others to have a lot of power and control over you. This way, you can blame them for where you are in life or you can hold others responsible for the fact that you may not have what you want. You might even try to find a really bad psychotherapist who will help you blame your parents for your lot in life and thereby keep you stuck in the role of the victim. Other suggestions for achieving your goals: cross your fingers, visit tarot card readers or astrologers, sit back and wait for chance encounters, and make sure to read your "horror"scopes daily.

3. PLAY IT REALLY, REALLY SAFE

Your motto should be: *Stay in my own world, trust no one, and resist letting others know me.* This will ensure that you stay safe in your little cocoon. You won't have to fool with the uncomfortable and messy details of relationship or the risks of rejection. Oh, sure, you will miss out on the thrills of intimacy and the rewards of companionship, but that's a small price to pay for your predictable and secure comfort zone.

4. GO WITH THE FLOW

Rather than choose to be proactive and methodical about the dating process, be reactive. That's right. Let things come to you and then respond accordingly. Avoid any semblance of purpose, intention, or direction—you don't want to try and tempt fate. Let love find you.

5. THANK YOUR "LUCKY STARS"

Finally, if love happens (by chance) to find you, go with it! Be content to have anyone who falls in that category of *playmate.* Your motto should be: *I'll take what I can get.* Don't be discriminating or judgmental about finding good character, and by all means, don't worry about spiritual or relational compatibility. Don't waste your time by trying to identify nonnegotiable qualities you must have in a mate. Just thank your lucky stars for whatever or whomever comes your way.

By now, you should be clear about what will keep you from finding The One. When your approach to dating is passive, reactive, haphazard, or superstitious, you will always come up short.

Conversely, when you choose to take responsibility and commit to balance God's leading and direction with a plan of action, you will be well on your way to finding the love of your life. Don't compromise or settle for less. Resolve to find a partner with whom you can connect in all three Love Zones. Stay in the quest, take action as needed, identify your love target, and—above all—enjoy the process along the way!

About the Authors

BEN YOUNG, M.Div., author and speaker, leads seminars on how to build successful dating relationships. He hosts *The Single Connection,* a nationally syndicated radio show, and is an associate pastor at the 30,000-member Second Baptist Church in Houston, Texas. Ben and Sam Adams coauthored the bestselling book *The Ten Commandments of Dating.*

SAMUEL ADAMS, Psy. D., is a licensed clinical psychologist. He earned a bachelor's degree from Baylor University, his master's from Western Seminary, and a doctorate from George Fox Graduate School of Clinical Psychology. He maintains a full-time counseling practice and is a relationship conference speaker. He and his wife, Julie, have three children. They reside in Austin, Texas.

For more dating advice . . .

The Ten Commandments of Dating
EZ Lesson Plan

he Ten Commandments of Dating EZ Lesson Plan is great to take the practical and fundamental laws from the book and dig a little deeper. It can be used in a small-group setting, at a retreat, as a Sunday school alternative, or for individual study.

The EZ Lesson Plan includes one video, an audio tape, and a facilitator's guide. Also available is *The Ten Commandments of Dating* Participant's Guide, which includes self-quizzes, Scripture references, and more, serves as a personal workbook as well as a means to in-depth group discussion.

EZ Lesson Plan
ISBN 0-7852-9619-0

Participant's Guide
0-7852-9621-2

To order any of the above resources, you can contact your local Christian bookstore or log on to www.benyoung.org or call 1-800-553-9772.

The Single Connection

*Y*ou will not want to miss America's only live talk show just for singles. *The Single Connection* is broadcast live, every Sunday night, from 9–11 PM CST. Host Ben Young and cohost Toni Richmond are in touch and outspoken on all the hot topics that singles really want to know about. Topics such as dating, sex, relationships, divorce, pornography, the new age movement, homosexuality, and many others.

Singles from across the country call in to voice their opinions or ask a questions. Each week proves that singles are not alone in what they want to know.

The Single Connection often has guest experts such as Dr. Laura Schlessinger, Elisabeth Elliot, Henry Cloud and John Townsend, Dr. Neil Clark Warren, Josh McDowell, John Eldredge, Josh Harris, Dr. Les Parrott, and others.

How can you listen to *The Single Connection*? Check out your local Christian radio station on Sunday nights or listen live at www.benyoung.org.

At **www.benyoung.org** you can also check out our resources at our online bookstore and listen to archived shows.

Host a Dating Conference
with Ben Young

THE ONE DATING CONFERENCE

Help your singles and students discover the three secrets of
finding a soul mate in this one-of-a-kind conference
with Ben Young.

THE 10 COMMANDMENTS OF DATING
CONFERENCE

Ben Young unpacks the time-tested biblical principles of
building successful relationships in this dynamic conference.

These conferences will help your singles or students
apply practical wisdom for biblical dating. It is a
great outreach to the singles in your community
and is appropriate for believers and seekers. If
you would like to host a conference for your
singles or student group, please contact Ben
Young at:

Single Life Ministries
6400 Woodway
Houston, TX 77057
713-365-2342
www.benyoung.org

Available January 2002

DEVOTIONS FOR DATING COUPLES

Building a Foundation
of Spiritual Intimacy

ISBN 0-7852-6749-2

LaVergne, TN USA
27 January 2011
214225LV00004B/21/P